Good enough to eat

Irene Wise

Contents

First published in 1982 by Octopus Books Limited
59 Grosvenor Street, London W1

ISBN 0 906320 93 3

Printed in England by Severn Valley Press Limited

INTRODUCTION

Most of us are aware that we should give more thought to eating the right sort of foods. It is not dull, time-consuming and anti-social to enjoy delicious, unrefined products, and eating well certainly doesn't mean living on expensive faddy foods from exclusive shops. Nor does it involve total changes in your diet and lifestyle, as the recipes in this book show. Just as it takes many years of bad eating habits to undermine your health, so it takes a little while to feel healthier by sticking to the right foods.

These recipes have been written to encourage an interesting and sensible style of eating. However, if you are on a special diet or receiving medical treatment, consult your doctor before substituting the suggestions and recipes in this book.

No complicated utensils are essential, but an electric blender and a pressure cooker are useful in many cases, although not vital.

Freshness

Do eat food that is as fresh as possible. Processed foods, which generally contain added sugar, salt and preservatives, will probably be more expensive than your own dishes prepared from fresh ingredients anyway. Try to eat a green leaf vegetable every day, preferably raw in a salad.

Instead of canned fruit, enjoy fresh and dried fruits. When buying dried fruit, try to avoid those packed with mineral oil or prepared with glucose or sulphur by checking the label.

Natural sugar

Everybody can cut down on how much sugar they eat. It is present in so many natural foods, such as fruit and some vegetables, that our bodies require little or no extra sugar. It is a misconception that by eating a highly sweetened food, such as chocolate,

when we feel tired, we provide the body with useful energy. The effect of this is to raise the blood sugar very fast. The body reacts by lowering it again rapidly, sometimes to lower levels than before, and the result is often a craving for even more sweet, sugary foods.

It's much better to eat fresh or dried fruit and get your sugar in its natural form, along with the vitamins and dietary fibre found with it.

If you want to add extra sweetness or bake cakes or puddings – use a little honey, or raw sugar which has been purified to a much lesser extent than white sugar and may still contain traces of minerals.

Use raw sugars for general cooking, and molasses for special baking recipes. Check the sugar packet label to ensure that the contents are raw cane sugar, thus avoiding the brown sugars which are just white sugar dyed brown.

Whole grain cereals

White flour is made from wheat by removing most of the outer layers and discarding them; or selling them back to us as bran! This white flour is therefore lower in dietary fibre, vitamins and minerals than flour made from the whole grain. The same applies to other cereals, such as rice.

Using wholegrain cereals ensures that you get all the value of the cereal, not only the vitamins and minerals but also the dietary fibre – a part of our diet which is increasingly being recognized as essential for health.

Use wholemeal flour to thicken soups and stews as well as for baking; change to wholemeal bread and substitute wholemeal pasta for the white type – all those foods have a delicious nutty flavour as well as supplying extra food value.

When eating rice choose brown, unpolished rice – it takes longer to cook but has much more flavour than the white variety – even in puddings. You can also use more unusual cereals such as cracked wheat or barley to add variety and interest to your meals.

Seasonings

Try to use salt only sparingly to bring out the flavour of the food and not to make it taste salty. Sea salt gives extra flavour to foods and may also supply small amounts of other minerals and trace elements. Use the coarse type for general purposes and fine sea salt, which can be sifted, for pastry-making and baking.

A little pepper or a few spices can add imagination to a simple dish. Use herbs to vary the flavour of food and you will probably find that less salt is necessary. Fresh herbs have a better flavour than dried and some herbs, such as parsley, which contains vitamin C, are available all year round.

Natural flavourings

Buy an essence rather than a chemical flavouring, and in the case of vanilla, the cheapest form of flavouring is a vanilla pod in a jar of raw brown sugar (page 70). Avoid artificial flavourings, which will be listed on the label of a product.

Yogurt

Yogurt is an easily digested source of milk protein and calcium which is simple to make (see page 8) and is a useful low-calorie ingredient.

Whenever possible choose plain yogurt rather than flavoured yogurt – the latter usually has artificial flavouring, colouring and preservatives added as well as a high proportion of sugar. If you like fruit yogurt, make your own delicious version by adding chopped fresh fruit, and a little honey.

Fats

Fats are a concentrated source of energy and because of this it is better not to have too much of any fat. Apart from helping the absorption of vitamins A, D, E and K, we also need a small amount of fat each day to provide linoleic acid, an 'essential' fatty acid which we cannot make ourselves.

The fat in foods can be either 'saturated' or 'unsaturated' or as in most foods, a mixture of both. The consumption of diets with a lot of saturated fat has been linked with high blood cholesterol levels and heart disease. Foods with a lot of this type of fat include cream, butter, cheese, egg yolks, suet, lard, fat on meat and hard margarines.

The other type of fats, containing mainly polyunsaturated fatty acids are of vegetable origin. Particularly high levels are found in some vegetable oils, such as sunflower, safflower and corn oils. Other vegetable oils, e.g. olive oil, are not especially polyunsaturated. If taken in sufficient quantity, the polyunsaturated oils can lower blood cholesterol, but there is as yet no evidence that this will prevent heart attacks.

The best policy is to keep your fat intake low – use recipes with a lot of fat as treats and instead get your energy from unrefined starchy foods such as cereals and potatoes.

Meat

Both meat and vegetarian diets can be healthy, in conjunction with sensible eating habits. However, it is now believed that we eat too much meat (and it's associated fat). As a change try serving more meals with less or no meat. Try basing occasional meals on pulse vegetables such as lentils or beans – these are rich in protein and dietary fibre.

Drink naturally

The best drink is probably water. Most canned and fizzy drinks, and commercial squashes are sweetened water with added artificial flavour and preservatives and they increase your sugar intake. Large amounts of stimulants such as tea, coffee and alcohol aren't particularly good for you either.

Try fresh fruit juices, or herb teas, sweetened with a little honey. Herb teas or tisanes have long been popular on the Continent, where they are often served in restaurants and cafés, too.

BREAKFAST

For a healthy start to the day, choose a breakfast from fresh fruit, natural yogurt, unprocessed cereals and wholegrain breads. Try to avoid processed and fried foods. By eating wholegrain foods you will be provided with a balance of nutrients that produce enough energy for the whole morning. The best kind of breakfast need not be large or involve lengthy preparation, but it is one that is low in fat and refined sugar.

If you like a cooked breakfast, eat a boiled or poached egg, grilled sausages, tomatoes or mushrooms on wholemeal toast, or kippers. Porridge is nutritious and when made with water it is low in calories too. Spread wholemeal toast with yeast extract and curd cheese, and use butter or margarine sparingly.

Fresh fruit salad

Metric	Imperial
2 oranges, peeled and segmented	2 oranges, peeled and segmented
2 apples, cored and sliced	2 apples, cored and sliced
2 pears, peeled, cored and chopped	2 pears, peeled, cored and chopped
100 g seedless grapes	4 oz seedless grapes
½ grapefruit, peeled and segmented	½ grapefruit, peeled and segmented
1–2 × 15 ml spoons Barbados sugar or clear honey	1–2 tablespoons Barbados sugar or clear honey
juice of 1 lemon	juice of 1 lemon
chopped mint, to garnish (optional)	chopped mint, to garnish (optional)

Preparation time: 5–10 minutes

To obtain the maximum benefit of the high vitamin C content of the fresh fruit the salad should be prepared just before eating.

Mix all the fruit together in a serving dish. Stir the sugar or honey into the lemon juice and pour it over the fruit. Scatter with mint leaves and serve with Natural Yogurt (page 8).

Variations:
Any particular fresh fruit in season may be included, such as peaches, cherries, blackberries, strawberries, melon, bananas, blackcurrants, mangoes, apricots or plums.
Substitute the juice of an orange for the sweetened lemon juice.

Fresh fruit salad; Muesli

Muesli

Metric	Imperial
225 g jumbo or rolled oats	8 oz jumbo or rolled oats
100 g wheat, barley or rye flakes	4 oz wheat, barley or rye flakes
50 g sesame seeds	2 oz sesame seeds
50 g sunflower seeds	2 oz sunflower seeds
100 g seedless raisins or sultanas	4 oz seedless raisins or sultanas
25 g pumpkin seeds	1 oz pumpkin seeds
225 g mixed dried fruit (bananas, apricots, peaches, figs, pears, dates, nectarines), chopped	8 oz mixed dried fruit (bananas, apricots, peaches, figs, pears, dates, nectarines), chopped
50 g mixed nuts (cashew nuts, hazelnuts, Brazil nuts), chopped	2 oz mixed nuts (cashew nuts, hazelnuts, Brazil nuts), chopped

Preparation time: 10 minutes

Pumpkin seeds are available from health food stores. If you keep a vanilla pod in the container with the muesli it will be delicately and naturally flavoured.

Combine all the ingredients and store in an airtight container.
The night before serving, soak 2 × 15 ml spoons/2 tablespoons muesli in 3 × 15 ml spoons/3 tablespoons milk for each person. The next morning, add a small banana, sliced and a tart apple, coarsely grated. Serve immediately with one of the following, or with a little malt extract mixed with milk.

Toppings:
Use 3 × 15 ml spoons/3 tablespoons cream, mixed with 1 × 5 ml spoon/1 teaspoon lemon juice and 1 × 15 ml spoon/1 tablespoon clear honey.
Use 3 × 15 ml spoons/3 tablespoons Natural Yogurt (page 8) mixed with 1 × 15 ml spoon/1 tablespoon honey and 1 × 5 ml spoon/1 teaspoon lemon juice.

Natural yogurt

Metric	Imperial
600 ml whole or skimmed milk	1 pint whole or skimmed milk
1 × 15 ml spoon live natural yogurt	1 tablespoon live natural yogurt

Preparation time: 5 minutes, plus 4–8 hours for setting
Cooking time: 5 minutes

Yogurt is the most easily digested of all dairy protein so it makes a healthy start to the day, served with cereal, or fresh or dried fruit. On its own it is delicious topped with a spoonful of honey and sprinkled with a few chopped nuts. When preparing it the whey should be drained off and this can be used in scones or soups.

Home-made yogurt can cost less than a third of commercial yogurt, but it is best to use a live yogurt, which contains *Lactobacillus bulgaricus*, as the basis for home-made yogurt. You do not need an electric yogurt maker; simply use a large wide-necked vacuum flask or earthenware container. However, it is worth investing in a cooking thermometer. Where a recipe in this book refers to natural yogurt, either this home-made variety or bought yogurt can be used.

Bring the milk to the boil in a saucepan and simmer for 2 minutes. Remove from the heat and allow to cool to just above blood heat or 38–54°C/100–130°F on a cooking thermometer. The temperature can be tested with the little finger if a thermometer is not available. It should be just comfortable to hold the finger in the milk for a count of 10.
Remove any skin from the milk and whisk in the yogurt. Pour the mixture into the flask and seal. Leave for at least 4 hours, or overnight. If using an earthenware container it should be wrapped in a towel and left in a warm, draught-free place such as the airing cupboard. Avoid leaving the yogurt to set for longer than 8 hours, as this tends to make the new yogurt rather sour.
Drain the watery whey from the top and reserve this for baking. Pour the set yogurt into a bowl or jug, cover and leave to cool completely. Store the yogurt in the refrigerator, where it should keep for up to one week. A fresh batch can be made from the home-made yogurt and this is most effective if it is less than 5 days old.

Dried fruit compôte

Metric	Imperial
100 g dried peaches	4 oz dried peaches
100 g dried pears	4 oz dried pears
100 g dried apricots	4 oz dried apricots
50 g seedless raisins or sultanas	2 oz seedless raisins or sultanas
50 g stoned dates	2 oz stoned dates
finely grated rind and juice of 1 orange	finely grated rind and juice of 1 orange
600 ml water	1 pint water

Preparation time: 5 minutes, plus 8–12 hours for soaking
Cooking time: 15 minutes

Put all the fruit into a bowl, add the orange rind and juice and water. Cover and soak for 8–12 hours.
Put the soaked fruit and any remaining liquid into a large saucepan and bring to the boil. Cover and simmer very gently for 15 minutes.
Serve hot or cold.

Natural yogurt; Dried fruit compôte; Honeyed cereal

Honeyed cereal

Metric
4 × 15 ml spoons
  sunflower or safflower
  oil
225 g clear honey
450 g jumbo or rolled
  oats, or wheat, rye or
  barley flakes
100 g mixed unsalted
  nuts, chopped
50 g sesame seeds
50 g dried peaches, pears
  or figs, chopped
50 g dried bananas,
  chopped
100 g sultanas or seedless
  raisins
50 g pumpkin seeds

Imperial
4 tablespoons sunflower
  or safflower
  oil
8 oz clear honey
1 lb jumbo or rolled oats,
  or wheat, rye or barley
  flakes
4 oz mixed unsalted nuts,
  chopped
2 oz seasame seeds
2 oz dried peaches, pears
  or figs, chopped
2 oz dried bananas,
  chopped
4 oz sultanas or seedless
  raisins
2 oz pumpkin seeds

Preparation time: 20 minutes
Cooking time: 20 minutes
Oven: 180°C, 350°F, Gas Mark 4

You can also use this mixture as a delicious filling for baked apples. If a vanilla pod is kept in the container the cereal will acquire a delicate vanilla flavour. Health food stores sell the pumpkin seeds.

Warm the oil in a roasting tin. Stir in the honey and oats or flakes. Add the nuts and sesame seeds and cook in a preheated oven for 20 minutes. Stir the mixture occasionally so that it browns evenly.
Remove from the oven. Allow to cool, then mix in the dried fruit and pumpkin seeds. Store in an airtight container.
Serve for breakfast with Natural Yogurt (page 8), whole or skimmed milk or buttermilk, and with fresh fruit.

Porridge

Metric	Imperial
175 g coarse or medium oatmeal, or rolled or jumbo oats	6 oz coarse or medium oatmeal, or rolled or jumbo oats
1.2 litres water	2 pints water
1 × 5 ml spoon sea salt	1 teaspoon sea salt

Preparation time: 5 minutes
Cooking time: 15–20 minutes

Porridge makes a warming and nutritious start to the day and if it is made with water it is surprisingly low in calories. If preferred, the oats can be soaked in the water overnight and the cooking time reduced to about 5 minutes.

Place the oatmeal or oats in a saucepan with the water and bring to the boil. Add the salt, cover and simmer gently for 15–20 minutes, stirring frequently. Serve with a little honey, molasses or Barbados sugar and top of the milk or Natural Yogurt (page 8). This is also a good accompaniment to Dried Fruit Compôte (page 8).

Variation:
Soak 100 g/4 oz sultanas or seedless raisins, or a few prunes, with the oats overnight. Cook as above.

Jug-cooked kippers

Metric	Imperial
4 kippers	4 kippers
50 g butter	2 oz butter

Preparation time: 5 minutes
Cooking time: 5 minutes

If possible buy undyed kippers from a good fishmonger or one that does his own smoking. Their flavour is much better.

Place the kippers in a large jug and pour on enough freshly boiled water so that all but the kippers' tails are covered. Leave for 3–5 minutes, then pull out the kippers by their tails. Serve with butter and accompanied by slices of Wholemeal Bread (page 12).

Herbed skinless sausages

Metric	Imperial
750 g belly of pork, rind removed, finely minced	1½ lb belly of pork, rind removed, finely minced
100 g fresh wholemeal breadcrumbs, moistened with a little water, or half lemon juice and half water	4 oz fresh wholemeal breadcrumbs, moistened with a little water, or half lemon juice and half water
1 egg (size 1 or 2), beaten	1 egg (size 1 or 2), beaten
finely grated rind of ½ lemon	finely grated rind of ½ lemon
1 × 1.25 ml spoon dried thyme	¼ teaspoon dried thyme
1 × 1.25 ml spoon dried savory	¼ teaspoon dried savory
1 × 1.25 ml spoon dried sage	¼ teaspoon dried sage
1 × 2.5 ml spoon sea salt	½ teaspoon sea salt
freshly ground black pepper	freshly ground black pepper
about 4 × 15 ml spoons wholemeal plain flour	about 4 tablespoons wholemeal plain flour
a little oil	a little oil

Preparation time: 15 minutes
Cooking time: 15 minutes

Many bought sausages contain a lot of fat which plumps them up and runs out during cooking. Commercial sausages may also contain chemical preservatives and colouring. This recipe makes eight substantial sausages, which with a squeeze of lemon and garnished with fresh parsley will also make a tasty supper dish. You can prepare these sausages the night before, but as they do not contain preservative, they should be kept in the refrigerator and eaten within 2–3 days.

Put all the ingredients, except the flour, in a large mixing bowl and mix evenly. Divide the mixture into eight portions and roll into fairly thick sausages about 10 cm/4 inches long. Sprinkle the flour and a little salt and pepper on to a board. Roll each sausage in the seasoned flour until well coated.
The best method of cooking is to grill the sausages. Brush the grill pan with a little oil to prevent the sausages sticking and cook them under a preheated grill for about 15 minutes. As they are thicker than most sausages make sure that they are cooked.

Jug-cooked kippers;
Herbed skinless sausages; Porridge

Quick wholemeal loaf or rolls

Preparation time: 15–20 minutes, plus 20 minutes for proving
Cooking time: 15 minutes, plus 30–40 minutes for a loaf or 15 minutes for rolls
Oven: 230°C, 450°F, Gas Mark 8;
      200°C, 400°F, Gas Mark 6

Metric
25 g fresh yeast or 15 g dried yeast
1 × 5 ml spoon Barbados sugar
about 300 ml lukewarm water
450 g plain wholemeal flour
1 × 5 ml spoon sea salt
1 × 15 ml spoon sunflower oil

To finish:
1 egg, beaten
2 × 5 ml spoons poppy seeds, cracked wheat or sesame seeds

Imperial
1 oz fresh yeast or ½ oz dried yeast
1 teaspoon Barbados sugar
about ½ pint lukewarm water
1 lb plain wholemeal flour
1 teaspoon sea salt
1 tablespoon sunflower oil

To finish:
1 egg, beaten
2 teaspoons poppy seeds, cracked wheat or sesame seeds

Grease a 1 kg/2 lb loaf tin (or a baking sheet, if making rolls) with oil, dust with a little flour and place in the oven turned to its lowest setting. Put the yeast into a small bowl with the sugar and stir in 150 ml/¼ pint of the warm water. Put the yeast mixture into the very cool oven and leave until frothy. Fresh yeast will take about 8 minutes to activate, dried yeast 10–15 minutes: if it does not become frothy by this time, it is too old and should be discarded. Put the flour and salt into a large mixing bowl and warm this bowl in the oven too.

When the yeast is activated, remove the bowls from the oven. Make a well in the centre of the dry ingredients and pour in the yeast mixture and oil. Gradually add the remaining water, stirring until the dough is sticky and soft, but not too wet. Depending upon the absorption of the flour it may be necessary to add up to 150 ml/¼ pint extra warm water.

Turn the dough on to a floured board and knead for about 10 minutes or until the dough is soft and elastic. Push the dough away from you with the palms of your hands, then draw it towards you with your fingertips, folding the dough over as you pull it back. Knead vigorously as this distributes the yeast and helps the bread to rise.

Put the kneaded dough into the prepared tin, or shape into 15 small rolls and place on the prepared baking sheet. Cover with a clean cloth, or put into a plastic bag, and leave to prove in a warm place for 50–60 minutes or until the dough has almost doubled in size.

Brush the loaf or rolls with the beaten egg and sprinkle with the poppy seeds, cracked wheat or sesame seeds. Bake towards the top of a preheated oven for 15 minutes, then reduce the temperature and bake for a further 30–40 minutes for a loaf, or about 15 minutes for rolls. The bread is cooked when it begins to shrink away from the sides of the tin and sounds hollow when the bottom of the loaf is tapped. Remove from the tin or baking sheet and cool on a wire tray.

Makes one 1 kg/2 lb loaf or 15 rolls

Variations for Quick Wholemeal Loaf and Rolls:
Wheatmeal loaf: Use plain wheatmeal flour for a less coarse loaf.

Wholemeal barley loaf: Use 225 g/8 oz barley flour with 225 g/8 oz wholemeal flour and finish with 2 × 5 ml spoons/2 teaspoons barley flakes.

Wholemeal rye loaf: Use 225 g/8 oz rye flour with 225 g/8 oz wholemeal flour and finish with 2 × 5 ml spoons/2 teaspoons caraway seeds.

Oatmeal loaf: Use 100 g/4 oz fine oatmeal with 350 g/12 oz wholemeal flour and finish with 2 × 5 ml spoons/2 teaspoons rolled oats.

Apricot and sunflower seed bread: Add 100 g/4 oz dried apricots, chopped, and 50 g/2 oz sunflower seeds to the flour before stirring in the yeast mixture, oil and remaining water. Sprinkle the loaf or rolls with sunflower seeds after glazing and bake as above. For a more savoury loaf, add only the sunflower seeds and omit the dried apricots.

Wholemeal bread; Fruit bran loaf

Fruit bran loaf

Metric	Imperial
150 g bran cereal	5 oz bran cereal
275 g mixed sultanas and seedless raisins	10 oz mixed sultanas and seedless raisins
300 ml whole or skimmed milk or buttermilk	½ pint whole or skimmed milk or buttermilk
150 g plain wholemeal flour	5 oz plain wholemeal flour
1 × 15 ml spoon baking powder	1 tablespoon baking powder
1 × 1.25 ml spoon ground mixed spice	¼ teaspoon ground mixed spice
grated rind of ½ orange (optional)	grated rind of ½ orange (optional)
1 egg (size 1 or 2), beaten	1 egg (size 1 or 2), beaten

Preparation time: 10 minutes, plus overnight soaking
Cooking time: 1 hour
Oven: 180°C, 350°F, Gas Mark 4

This bread is very quick and simple to prepare. Although it is delicious sliced and spread with butter it is fruity enough to serve as a cake.

Put the bran cereal, dried fruit and milk or buttermilk in a large mixing bowl, cover with a plate and leave to soak overnight.
The next day, sift the flour, baking powder and spice into the bowl, then tip in any bran left in the sieve. Add the orange rind, if used. Make a well in the centre, add the egg and mix thoroughly.
Put the mixture into a greased 1 kg/2 lb loaf tin. Bake in a preheated oven for 1 hour or until a skewer inserted into the centre of the loaf comes out clean. Loosen the loaf with a palette knife and turn out on to a wire tray to cool.

SOUPS AND LIGHT MEALS

Home-made soup is simple to prepare and nutritious. The quality of the stock plays an important part and it is easy to make your own and quick, too, especially if you have a pressure cooker. If you don't have time to make your own simply use water, or water mixed with a little yeast extract or a few herbs. Stock cubes are very highly flavoured and contain a lot of salt, so it is best to dissolve half a stock cube in as much water as usually given for a whole one. Croûtons made from wholemeal bread and sprinkled with sea salt make a good addition to many soups.

Although many of us tend to eat our largest meal in the evening, this provides the body with a lot of work overnight to assimilate the nutrients. Therefore, it is better to eat a lighter supper. The recipes in this chapter are also ideal for weekends and lunches.

Lettuce soup with mint

Metric	Imperial
15 g butter	½ oz butter
1 large onion, peeled and chopped	1 large onion, peeled and chopped
2 large lettuces, outside leaves only	2 large lettuces, outside leaves only
5–6 fresh sorrel or spinach leaves, chopped (optional)	5–6 fresh sorrel or spinach leaves, chopped (optional)
3 medium potatoes, peeled and cubed	3 medium potatoes, peeled and cubed
600 ml chicken or vegetable Stock (page 16) or water	1 pint chicken or vegetable Stock (page 16) or water
600 ml milk	1 pint milk
sea salt	sea salt
freshly ground black pepper	freshly ground black pepper
1 egg yolk	1 egg yolk
2 × 15 ml spoons single cream or top of the milk	2 tablespoons single cream or top of the milk
4–5 fresh mint leaves, chopped, or 1 × 5 ml spoon dried mint	4–5 fresh mint leaves chopped, or 1 teaspoon dried mint
finely chopped fresh mint, to garnish	finely chopped fresh mint, to garnish

Preparation time: 10–15 minutes
Cooking time: 20 minutes

This is a delicate soup, so take care not to add too much salt or pepper, or to overcook it. It is best made with crisp lettuces, such as Webb or Cos, and as only the outer leaves are used, the young hearts can be used in a salad.

Melt the butter in a saucepan, add the onion and fry until transparent. Add the lettuce and sorrel or spinach leaves, if used, cover and cook gently for a further 5 minutes. Stir in the potatoes, stock or water, milk and salt and pepper, and bring to the boil. Cover and simmer for 15–20 minutes or until the potato is tender.
Sieve or blend the soup to a purée. Stir the egg yolk and cream or top of the milk together in a cup and, if using a blender, add them to the last batch of soup being puréed. Alternatively, return the soup to the rinsed pan and stir in the yolk and cream or milk mixture. Taste and adjust the seasoning and add the mint. Heat through but do not allow the soup to boil.
Serve very hot, garnished with more mint, and with crusty Wholemeal Bread (page 12), or croûtons.

Stuffed cabbage with bacon and chestnuts;
Lettuce soup with mint

Stuffed cabbage with bacon and chestnuts

Metric	Imperial
450 g chestnuts	1 lb chestnuts
1 large firm green cabbage	1 large firm green cabbage
5 streaky bacon rashers, rind removed, quartered	5 streaky bacon rashers, rind removed, quartered
sea salt	sea salt
freshly ground black pepper	freshly ground black pepper
25 g butter, cut into pieces	1 oz butter, cut into pieces
about 300 ml Stock (page 16) or water	about ½ pint Stock (page 16) or water

Preparation time: 40 minutes
Cooking time: 35 minutes
Oven: 180°C, 350°F, Gas Mark 4

For convenience, substitute dried chestnuts for fresh in this recipe. Pour boiling water over them and leave to soak overnight. Simmer in stock or water for 1½–2 hours or until tender, then drain and use as for fresh.

Place the chestnuts on a chopping board and with a sharp knife make a cut from just above the middle down to the pointed end. Cook the chestnuts in boiling water for 10–15 minutes. Remove the chestnuts individually and, protecting your fingers with a cloth or oven glove, peel the shell away with a knife. The chestnuts can still be used if they break into pieces. If the skin does not come away easily, return the chestnuts to the boiling water for a few more minutes.
Blanch the cabbage in boiling water for 5 minutes. Drain and, if possible, strip away whole leaves without splitting them. Lay each leaf on the chopping board, and place a piece of bacon and 1–2 chestnuts in each. Use two leaves together if they are very delicate. Roll up each leaf like a parcel and place, with the overlapping edge underneath, in a well greased shallow ovenproof dish. Pack the parcels in tightly, in one layer if possible. Any leftover whole chestnuts can be pressed in between the parcels. Sprinkle with a little salt and pepper and add the butter. Pour in enough of the stock or water to come 5 mm/¼ inch up the parcels. Cover with a lid or foil, and cook in a preheated oven for 25 minutes. Uncover and cook for a further 10 minutes.
Serve with Fresh Tomato Sauce (page 30) or simply with the pan juices, and Boiled Brown Rice (page 34).

Stock

Preparation time: 5 minutes
Cooking time: 3–4 hours

Metric	Imperial
1 chicken carcass (or turkey, duck, game bird carcass), or ¾–1 kg beef bones (shin, marrow), chopped	*1 chicken carcass (or turkey, duck, game bird carcass), or 1½–2 lb beef bones (shin, marrow), chopped*
1 leek, chopped (optional)	*1 leek, chopped (optional)*
1 onion, peeled and stuck with 2–3 cloves	*1 onion, peeled and stuck with 2–3 cloves*
2 carrots, scraped	*2 carrots, scraped*
1 celery stick	*1 celery stick*
1 bay leaf	*1 bay leaf*
1 parsley sprig	*1 parsley sprig*
few black peppercorns	*few black peppercorns*
sea salt	*sea salt*

Chicken giblets, excluding the liver, also add flavour to stock, as do bacon rinds. However, do not mix both cooked and uncooked meat bones. Chicken stock enhances the flavour of most vegetable soups, and if you have not recently cooked a chicken, it's quite economical to buy a few wings to simmer in your stock instead of the carcass. If using a pressure cooker allow about 45 minutes' cooking time.

Put the carcass or bones into a large saucepan, cover with cold water and bring to the boil. Skim well, then add all the remaining ingredients. Simmer very gently until the liquid is well reduced, then strain into a bowl or jug. Allow to cool, then skim off all the fat. Keep in the refrigerator and use within 3 days.

Variation:
Vegetable stock : Omit the carcass or bones and leek, and use 450 g/1 lb carrots and 450 g/1 lb onions with the celery, herbs and seasonings. Add other vegetables, such as turnips or mushrooms, but do not add potatoes, which tend to make the stock cloudy.
Use instead of beef or chicken stock, especially where the other ingredients in a recipe suit a lighter stock.

Stock ; Sweetcorn soup ; White bean soup

Sweetcorn soup

Metric	Imperial
25 g butter	1 oz butter
3 streaky bacon rashers (about 75 g), rind removed, diced	3 streaky bacon rashers (about 3 oz), rind removed, diced
1 onion, peeled and chopped	1 onion, peeled and chopped
1 garlic clove, peeled and chopped	1 garlic clove, peeled and chopped
1 carrot, scraped and chopped	1 carrot, scraped and chopped
1 celery stick, chopped	1 celery stick, chopped
1.75 litres chicken Stock (page 16)	3 pints chicken Stock (page 16)
450 g potatoes, peeled and cubed	1 lb potatoes, peeled and cubed
1 × 350 g can sweetcorn, drained	1 × 12 oz can sweetcorn, drained
sea salt	sea salt
freshly ground black pepper	freshly ground black pepper
2 × 15 ml spoons chopped fresh parsley	2 tablespoons chopped fresh parsley
½ green pepper, cored, seeded and thinly sliced	½ green pepper, cored, seeded and thinly sliced

Preparation time: 15 minutes
Cooking time: 15–20 minutes

Melt the butter in a large saucepan, add the bacon and fry until golden and just crisp. Remove the bacon with a slotted spoon and set on one side. Add the onion and garlic to the pan and fry gently in the butter and bacon fat until softened. Add the carrot and celery and fry for a further minute.

Add the chicken stock, potatoes and two thirds of the sweetcorn with salt and pepper. Bring to the boil, skimming if necessary, and simmer for 15 minutes or until the potatoes are soft.

Allow to cool for a few minutes, then purée in a mouli légumes or blender. Return to the rinsed pan and stir in the parsley, green pepper, reserved bacon and remaining sweetcorn. Reheat gently.
Serves 6

White bean soup

Metric	Imperial
50 g butter or 4 × 15 ml spoons olive oil	2 oz butter or 4 tablespoons olive oil
1 onion, peeled and chopped	1 onion, peeled and chopped
1 garlic clove, peeled and chopped	1 garlic clove, peeled and chopped
4 streaky bacon rashers, rind removed, chopped (optional)	4 streaky bacon rashers, rind removed, chopped (optional)
3 potatoes, peeled and chopped	3 potatoes, peeled and chopped
1 carrot, scraped and chopped	1 carrot, scraped and chopped
100 g dried haricot beans, soaked overnight and drained	4 oz dried haricot beans, soaked overnight and drained
about 1.2 litres Stock (page 16) or water	about 2 pints Stock (page 16) or water
1 parsley sprig	1 parsley sprig
1 bay leaf	1 bay leaf
1 × 15 ml spoon dried chervil	1 tablespoon dried chervil
freshly ground black pepper	freshly ground black pepper
sea salt	sea salt
1 garlic clove, peeled and crushed	1 garlic clove, peeled and crushed
2 × 15 ml spoons chopped fresh parsley, to garnish	2 tablespoons chopped fresh parsley, to garnish

Preparation time: 15 minutes, plus overnight soaking
Cooking time: about 2½ hours

Melt half of the butter, or heat half of the oil, in a large saucepan. Add the onion, garlic and half the bacon and fry for 5 minutes. Add two of the potatoes and the carrot, cover tightly and cook over a low heat for 10 minutes, shaking the pan occasionally.

Add the beans, stock or water, sprig of parsley, bay leaf, chervil and pepper to taste. Do not add salt at this stage or the beans will not soften. Cover, bring to the boil, boil for 10 minutes then simmer for 2 hours. Remove the bay leaf and purée the soup to a smooth cream in a blender. Return to the saucepan. Dilute with more stock or water if the soup seems a little too thick. Taste and adjust the seasoning. Reheat gently. Dice and put the remaining potato into a small saucepan, cover with cold water and bring to the boil. Boil for 2 minutes then drain. Melt the remaining butter or heat the remaining oil in a frying pan. Add the potato and remaining bacon and fry until golden brown. Stir in the garlic with salt and pepper to taste. Serve the soup hot, garnished with the bacon and potato mixture, and parsley sprinkled on top.

Cabbage and potato soup

Metric	Imperial
15 g butter	½ oz butter
1 onion, peeled and chopped	1 onion, peeled and chopped
1 leek, finely chopped	1 leek, finely chopped
1 carrot, scraped and diced	1 carrot, scraped and diced
175 g white or green cabbage, cored and shredded	6 oz white or green cabbage, cored and shredded
470 g potatoes, peeled and diced	1 lb potatoes, peeled and diced
1.2 litres Stock (page 16) or water	2 pints Stock (page 16) or water
1 parsley sprig	1 parsley sprig
sea salt	sea salt
freshly ground black pepper	freshly ground black pepper
1 × 5 ml spoon caraway seeds	1 teaspoon caraway seeds

To garnish:

Metric	Imperial
150 ml soured cream	¼ pint soured cream
2 × 15 ml spoons chopped fresh parsley	2 tablespoons chopped fresh parsley

Preparation time: 10–15 minutes
Cooking time: 30 minutes

This soup is made from simple and inexpensive ingredients yet tastes absolutely marvellous. It is very, very thick and with French bread it is filling enough to be a main course.

Melt the butter in a large saucepan, add the onion and fry until transparent. Add the leek and carrot, cover the pan tightly, and fry gently for about 10 minutes. Shake the pan occasionally to ensure that the vegetables do not stick to the bottom.
Add the cabbage and potatoes, cover with the stock or water and add the parsley sprig and salt and pepper. Bring to the boil, cover and simmer for about 20 minutes or until the carrot and potatoes are very tender.
Stir in the caraway seeds and taste and adjust the seasoning. Pour into a warmed tureen or individual bowls and serve with a swirl of soured cream and a sprinkling of parsley.
Serves 6–8

Winter pea soup; Jerusalem artichoke soup;
Cabbage and potato soup

Jerusalem artichoke soup

Metric	Imperial
15 g butter	½ oz butter
1 onion, peeled and chopped	1 onion, peeled and chopped
1 garlic clove, peeled and chopped	1 garlic clove, peeled and chopped
1 large carrot, peeled and chopped	1 large carrot, peeled and chopped
750 g Jerusalem artichokes, thinly peeled and chopped	1½ lb Jerusalem artichokes, thinly peeled and chopped
1 medium potato, peeled and chopped	1 medium potato, peeled and chopped
600 ml chicken Stock (page 16)	1 pint chicken Stock (page 16)
1 parsley sprig	1 parsley sprig
1 bay leaf	1 bay leaf
sea salt	sea salt
freshly ground black pepper	freshly ground black pepper
600 ml milk	1 pint milk
1 × 1.25 ml spoon grated nutmeg	¼ teaspoon grated nutmeg
chopped fresh parsley, to garnish	chopped fresh parsley, to garnish

Preparation time: 25–30 minutes
Cooking time: 30 minutes

Jerusalem artichokes have a delicate flavour so it is best to use home-made stock, if possible.

Melt the butter in a large saucepan, add the onion and fry until transparent. Add the garlic and carrot and cook for 2–3 minutes longer. Add the artichokes and potato, cover with the stock and bring to the boil. Add the parsley, bay leaf and a little salt and pepper. Cover and simmer for 20 minutes.
Remove the bay leaf. Sieve or purée the soup in a blender with the milk and return it to the rinsed pan. Stir in the nutmeg. Reheat gently. Taste and adjust the seasoning.
Serve very hot, garnished with a little parsley and with wholemeal croûtons or crusty, warm Wholemeal Bread (page 12).

Winter pea soup

Metric	Imperial
350 g dried split green peas, rinsed	12 oz dried split green peas, rinsed
2.5 litres cold water	4½ pints cold water
1 pig's trotter (soaked overnight, if salted)	1 pig's trotter (soaked overnight, if salted)
25 g butter	1 oz butter
50 g streaky bacon rashers, rind removed, chopped	2 oz streaky bacon rashers, rind removed, chopped
1 onion, peeled and chopped	1 onion, peeled and chopped
2 carrots, scraped and chopped	2 carrots, scraped and chopped
2 leeks, chopped	2 leeks, chopped
1 turnip, peeled and chopped	1 turnip, peeled and chopped
1 celery stick, chopped	1 celery stick, chopped
few celery leaves	few celery leaves
sea salt	sea salt
freshly ground black pepper	freshly ground black pepper
3–4 frankfurters or bockwurst, sliced (optional)	3–4 frankfurters or bockwurst, sliced (optional)

Preparation time: 15–20 minutes, plus soaking time (optional)
Cooking time: 4¼ hours

This improves in flavour when made the day before, but because it will have thickened it should be diluted with a little more water when reheated. It is preferable to soak the split green peas for 2 hours before using. Do not add the frankfurters or bockwurst until just before serving.

Drain the peas, if soaked, and put into a large saucepan. Pour over the cold water, cover and bring to the boil, boil for 10 minutes, then allow to simmer for 1 hour. Add the pig's trotter, cover again and simmer for a further 2½ hours. Skim once or twice during the cooking time.
Towards the end of the cooking time, melt the butter in a frying pan, add the bacon and onion and fry for 5 minutes, stirring frequently. Stir in the carrots, leeks, turnip, celery and celery leaves, then cover tightly and cook gently for a further 10 minutes. Shake the pan occasionally to prevent sticking.
Add the vegetable mixture to the peas and cook, stirring occasionally, for 45 minutes or until the peas are very soft. Remove the pig's trotter. Skim the soup and purée in a blender. Return it to the rinsed pan, reheat and add salt and pepper to taste. Stir in the frankfurters or bockwurst and heat through thoroughly.

Fish and vegetable soup

Metric	Imperial
15 g butter	½ oz butter
1 onion, peeled and finely chopped	1 onion, peeled and finely chopped
2 leeks, chopped	2 leeks, chopped
1 large carrot, scraped and diced	1 large carrot, scraped and diced
3 large potatoes, peeled and diced	3 large potatoes, peeled and diced
100 g peas	4 oz peas
600 ml boiling water	1 pint boiling water
1 × 1.25 ml spoon demerara sugar	¼ teaspoon demerara sugar
1 parsley sprig	1 parsley sprig
sea salt	sea salt
freshly ground black pepper	freshly ground black pepper
750 g fresh haddock or hake, on the bone	1½ lb fresh haddock or hake, on the bone
600 ml milk	1 pint milk

To garnish:

2 × 15 ml spoons chopped fresh parsley	2 tablespoons chopped fresh parsley
2 × 15 ml spoons chopped fresh chives	2 tablespoons chopped fresh chives

Preparation time: 10–15 minutes
Cooking time: about 35 minutes

Melt the butter in a large saucepan, add the onion and fry until transparent. Add the leeks and carrot, cover and fry gently for about 3 minutes. Add the potatoes, peas (if using fresh ones), boiling water, sugar, parsley sprig and salt and pepper. Cover and cook for 10 minutes. Add the fish and simmer for a further 10 minutes or until tender. Remove the fish to a plate. Pour in the milk and bring back to the boil. Add frozen peas, if used. Allow the soup to simmer gently while flaking the fish, removing any skin and bones. Add the flaked fish to the soup and heat through.

Lamb broth

Metric	Imperial
1 large meaty uncooked lamb bone	1 large meaty uncooked lamb bone
2 litres cold water	3½ pints cold water
50 g dried butter beans, soaked overnight and drained	2 oz dried butter beans, soaked overnight and drained
50 g pot barley, rinsed	2 oz pot barley, rinsed
1 onion, peeled and finely chopped	1 onion, peeled and finely chopped
2 carrots, scraped and diced	2 carrots, scraped and diced
1 parsnip, peeled and diced	1 parsnip, peeled and diced
2 leeks, finely chopped	2 leeks, finely chopped
1 turnip, peeled and diced	1 turnip, peeled and diced
1 celery stick, chopped	1 celery stick, chopped
few celery leaves, chopped	few celery leaves, chopped
2 × 15 ml spoons chopped fresh parsley	2 tablespoons chopped fresh parsley
sea salt	sea salt
freshly ground black pepper	freshly ground black pepper
1 × 15 ml spoon tomato purée	1 tablespoon tomato purée
dash of Worcestershire sauce	dash of Worcestershire sauce

Preparation time: 15 minutes, plus overnight soaking
Cooking time: 2¾ hours

It is preferable to soak pot barley overnight although it can be cooked straight away. If you do not soak it, the soup may need to be simmered a little longer.

Put the bone into a large saucepan and cover with the cold water. Bring to the boil, and skim. Add the butter beans, cover, boil for 10 minutes and then simmer for 1¾ hours.
Skim the stock if necessary, then add the pot barley, all the vegetables, the parsley and salt and pepper. Cover and simmer for a further 45 minutes or until the beans and barley are soft.
Remove the bone, scrape off the meat, cut into small pieces and return to the soup. Stir in the tomato purée and Worcestershire sauce. Serve piping hot.

Smoked haddock flan

Metric

175 g plain wholemeal
  flour
1 × 1.25 ml spoon fine sea
  salt
40 g butter
40 g lard or vegetable
  fat
about 3 × 15 ml spoons
  cold water

Filling:

225 g smoked haddock
  fillets
300 ml milk
15 g butter
1 onion, peeled and finely
  chopped
1 red pepper, cored,
  seeded and chopped
2 × 15 ml spoons chopped
  fresh parsley
2 eggs
1 egg yolk
dash of Tabasco sauce
sea salt
freshly ground black
  pepper
50 g Cheddar cheese,
  grated

Imperial

6 oz plain wholemeal
  flour
$\frac{1}{4}$ teaspoon fine sea
  salt
$1\frac{1}{2}$ oz butter
$1\frac{1}{2}$ oz lard or vegetable
  fat
about 3 tablespoons cold
  water

Filling:

8 oz smoked haddock
  fillets
$\frac{1}{2}$ pint milk
$\frac{1}{2}$ oz butter
1 onion, peeled and finely
  chopped
1 red pepper, cored
  seeded and chopped
2 tablespoons chopped
  fresh parsley
2 eggs
1 egg yolk
dash of Tabasco sauce
sea salt
freshly ground black
  pepper
2 oz Cheddar cheese,
  grated

Preparation time: 15–20 minutes
Cooking time: about 55 minutes
Oven: 200°C, 400°F, Gas Mark 6;
     190°C, 375°F, Gas Mark 5

Sift the flour and salt into a large mixing bowl and tip in any bran left in the sieve. Rub in the fats until the mixture resembles fine breadcrumbs. Add just enough cold water to bind to a firm dough. Wrap in greaseproof paper and leave to rest in the refrigerator for at least 10 minutes.

Roll out the dough on a floured board and use to line a 20–23 cm/8–9 inch flan tin. Lightly prick the base and bake blind in a preheated oven for about 15 minutes. Meanwhile, put the haddock into a saucepan, pour on the milk and bring to the boil. Poach gently for about 10 minutes. Strain the milk into a bowl and flake the fish, removing any bones.

Melt the butter in a frying pan, add the onion and fry until transparent. Add the red pepper and fry for a further 1 minute. Allow to cool slightly, then spread the mixture in the pastry case. Add the flaked haddock and sprinkle with the parsley.

Beat the eggs and egg yolk into the strained milk and add the Tabasco sauce and salt and pepper to taste. Pour into the pastry case and sprinkle over the grated cheese. Reduce the oven temperature and cook the flan in the oven for about 35 minutes, or until the filling is lightly set and the top browned. Serve hot or cold with baked jacket potatoes and a tomato salad or Carrot and Watercress Salad with Orange (page 61).

Fish and vegetable soup; Lamb broth;
Smoked haddock flan

Lentil soup with coconut

Metric	Imperial
2 × 15 ml spoons oil	2 tablespoons oil
1 onion, peeled and chopped	1 onion, peeled and chopped
1–2 garlic cloves, peeled and chopped	1–2 garlic cloves, peeled and chopped
1½ × 5 ml spoons cumin seeds or ground cumin	1½ teaspoons cumin seeds or ground cumin
4 cardamoms or 1 × 1.25 ml spoon ground cardamom	4 cardamoms or ¼ teaspoon ground cardamom
1 carrot, scraped and chopped	1 carrot, scraped and chopped
1 × 5 ml spoon ground turmeric	1 teaspoon ground turmeric
175 g yellow lentils, rinsed thoroughly	6 oz yellow lentils, rinsed thoroughly
1.5 litres chicken Stock (page 16)	2½ pints chicken Stock (page 16)
2 bay leaves	2 bay leaves
1 × 15 ml spoon chopped fresh coriander leaves or 1 × 5 ml spoon ground coriander	1 tablespoon chopped fresh coriander leaves or 1 teaspoon ground coriander
sea salt	sea salt
freshly ground black pepper	freshly ground black pepper
40 g creamed coconut, cut into small pieces	1½ oz creamed coconut, cut into small pieces
1 × 15 ml spoon tomato purée	1 tablespoon tomato purée
few chopped fresh coriander leaves, to garnish	few chopped fresh coriander leaves, to garnish

Preparation time: 15 minutes
Cooking time: about 1 hour

Heat the oil in a large, deep saucepan, add the onion and garlic and fry for 2 minutes. If using whole spices, crush the cumin seeds and cardamoms together in a cup using the back of a spoon, or use a pestle and mortar. Discard the cardamom husks. Add the crushed or ground cumin and cardamom to the onion and garlic with the carrot and turmeric, and fry for 2 minutes.
Add the lentils, stock, bay leaves and coriander. Bring to the boil slowly, then add salt and pepper. Cover and simmer for 45–60 minutes or until the lentils are soft. Add the creamed coconut and stir until melted. Stir in the tomato purée. Remove the bay leaves and purée the soup in a blender. Return it to the rinsed pan and reheat gently. Taste and adjust the seasoning and serve very hot, garnished with a few chopped coriander leaves.

Sweetcorn fritters

Metric	Imperial
6 × 15 ml spoons plain wholemeal flour	6 tablespoons plain wholemeal flour
1½ × 5 ml spoons baking powder	1½ teaspoons baking powder
1 × 2.5 ml spoon fine sea salt	½ teaspoon fine sea salt
freshly ground black pepper	freshly ground black pepper
1 × 350 g can sweetcorn kernels, drained	1 × 12 oz can sweetcorn kernels, drained
1 × 5 ml spoon clear honey	1 teaspoon clear honey
3 eggs, separated	3 eggs, separated
150 ml Natural Yogurt (page 8)	¼ pint Natural Yogurt (page 8)
2 × 15 ml spoons chopped fresh parsley	2 tablespoons chopped fresh parsley
a little oil or melted butter for frying	a little oil or melted butter for frying

Preparation time: 10 minutes, plus 15 minutes for the batter to stand
Cooking time: 5–10 minutes

The batter for these fritters may be prepared up to one hour in advance.

Sift the flour, baking powder and salt into a large mixing bowl and tip in any bran left in the sieve. Add pepper, make a well in the centre and add the sweetcorn, honey, egg yolks, yogurt and 1 × 15 ml spoon/1 tablespoon of the parsley. Stir until well mixed.
Beat the egg whites until very stiff. Fold them into the sweetcorn mixture and set aside for 15 minutes.
Brush a frying pan with a little oil or melted butter and heat gently. Drop in 2–3 large spoonfuls of the batter and fry for 2 minutes or until the underside is brown. Turn and brown the other side. Remove from the pan and keep hot while you fry the remaining fritters.
Sprinkle with the remaining parsley and serve hot with Fresh Tomato Sauce (page 30) and accompanied by a green salad. These fritters may also be served with Hamburgers (page 41) and grilled bacon.
Makes about 12 small fritters

Variation:
Omit the freshly ground black pepper and parsley, and serve with honey for an unusual dessert.

Carrot soup

Metric

15 g butter
1 large onion, peeled and
  chopped
1 × 15 ml spoon plain
  wholemeal flour
450 g carrots, peeled and
  chopped
2 celery sticks, chopped
1.2 litres Stock (page
  16) or water
1 parsley sprig
1 bay leaf
sea salt
freshly ground black
  pepper
pinch of demerara sugar
  (optional)
2 × 15 ml spoons single
  cream
1 × 1.25 ml spoon grated
  nutmeg
chopped fresh parsley

Imperial

½ oz butter
1 large onion, peeled and
  chopped
1 tablespoon plain
  wholemeal flour
1 lb carrots, peeled and
  chopped
2 celery sticks, chopped
2 pints Stock (page 16)
  or water
1 parsley sprig
1 bay leaf
sea salt
freshly ground black
  pepper
pinch of demerara sugar
  (optional)
2 tablespoons single
  cream
¼ teaspoon grated
  nutmeg
chopped fresh parsley

Preparation time: 15 minutes
Cooking time: 35 minutes

Melt the butter in a large saucepan, add the onion and fry gently until transparent. Stir in the flour and cook for 2 minutes. Add the carrots, celery, stock or water, parsley, bay leaf and salt and pepper. Add a pinch of sugar if the carrots are not young and sweet. Bring to the boil, cover and simmer for 25–30 minutes or until the carrots are soft. Remove the bay leaf.

Sieve or blend the soup to a purée and return it to the rinsed pan. Reheat gently, then stir in the cream, nutmeg and plenty of chopped parsley. Taste and adjust the seasoning, then serve. Hand round wholemeal croûtons separately, or warm, crusty Wholemeal Bread (page 12).

Carrot soup; Sweetcorn fritters; Lentil soup with coconut

Spinach flan

Preparation time: 20–30 minutes
Cooking time: 45 minutes
Oven: 200°C, 400°F, Gas Mark 6;
190°C, 375°F, Gas Mark 5

Metric
175 g plain wholemeal
flour
1 × 1.25 ml spoon fine sea
salt
40 g vegetable margarine
or butter
40 g lard
about 3 × 15 ml spoons
cold water

Filling:
15 g butter
1 onion, peeled and finely
chopped
1 garlic clove, peeled and
chopped
500–750 g spinach,
trimmed and chopped
3 eggs (size 1 or 2)
225 g cottage or curd
cheese
150 ml Natural Yogurt
(page 8)
¼ teaspoon nutmeg
sea salt
freshly ground black
pepper
25 g Cheddar or
Parmesan cheese,
grated
1 × 1.25 ml spoon paprika

Imperial
6 oz plain wholemeal
flour
¼ teaspoon fine sea
salt
1½ oz vegetable
margarine or butter
1½ oz lard
about 3 tablespoons cold
water

Filling:
½ oz butter
1 onion, peeled and finely
chopped
1 garlic clove, peeled and
chopped
1¼–1½ lb spinach,
trimmed and chopped
3 eggs (size 1 or 2)
8 oz cottage or curd
cheese
¼ pint Natural Yogurt
(page 8)
1 × 1.25 ml spoon nutmeg
sea salt
freshly ground black
pepper
1 oz Cheddar or
Parmesan cheese,
grated
¼ teaspoon paprika

Sift the flour and salt into a large mixing bowl and tip in any bran left in the sieve. Rub in the fats until the mixture resembles fine breadcrumbs. Add just enough cold water to bind to a firm dough. Wrap in greaseproof paper and leave to rest in the refrigerator for at least 10 minutes.

Roll out the dough on a floured board and use to line a well-greased 23 cm/9 inch flan tin. Lightly prick the base and bake blind in a preheated oven for about 15 minutes.

Meanwhile, prepare the filling. Melt the butter in a saucepan, add the onion and garlic and fry until transparent. Add the spinach, cover tightly and cook gently for 10 minutes: no extra water should be needed. Remove from the heat and drain off the excess liquid. Cool slightly.

Beat the eggs with the curd cheese, yogurt, nutmeg and salt and pepper.

Allow the pastry case to cool slightly, then line with the spinach mixture. Pour over the yogurt mixture. Scatter with the grated cheese and sprinkle with the paprika. Reduce the oven temperature and cook the flan in a preheated oven for about 30 minutes.

Serve hot, warm or cold, with baked potatoes and a salad, such as Tomato and Avocado Salad (page 58) or Wholewheat Salad with Coriander (page 61).

Makes one 23 cm/9 inch flan

Spinach flan; Stuffed green peppers;
Watercress soufflé

Stuffed green peppers

Preparation time: 15 minutes
Cooking time: 1¼–1½ hours
Oven: 200°C, 400°F, Gas Mark 6

Metric	Imperial
100 g long-grain brown rice	4 oz long-grain brown rice
300 ml Stock (page 16) or water	½ pint Stock (page 16) or water
2 × 15 ml spoons olive oil	2 tablespoons olive oil
4 large or 8 small green peppers	4 large or 8 small green peppers
1 onion, peeled and chopped	1 onion, peeled and chopped
1 garlic clove, peeled and chopped	1 garlic clove, peeled and chopped
25 g pine nuts or blanched almonds, chopped	1 oz pine nuts or blanched almonds, chopped
225 g mushrooms, chopped	8 oz mushrooms, chopped
1 × 2.5 ml spoon dried oregano	½ teaspoon dried oregano
1 × 1.25 ml spoon dried basil	¼ teaspoon dried basil
sea salt	sea salt
freshly ground black pepper	freshly ground black pepper
4 tomatoes, skinned and chopped, or 1 × 225 g can tomatoes	4 tomatoes, skinned and chopped, or 1 × 8 oz can tomatoes
1 × 15 ml spoon tomato purée	1 tablespoon tomato purée
1 × 5 ml spoon Pesto (page 31) (optional)	1 teaspoon Pesto (page 31) (optional)
75 g Cheddar cheese, grated	3 oz Cheddar cheese, grated

Put the rice in a saucepan with the stock or lightly salted boiling water with a few drops of oil added. Cover tightly and cook gently for 35–40 minutes. Uncover and cook for a further 5–10 minutes or until all the liquid has been absorbed.

Meanwhile, prepare the peppers. Cut off their tops, and take a thin slice off their bases, if necessary, so that they will stand upright. Scoop out the cores and seeds, then blanch the peppers in lightly salted boiling water for 15 minutes. Rinse in cold water and drain.

Heat the remaining oil in a frying pan, add the onion and fry until transparent. Add the garlic and pine nuts or almonds, and fry for 2 minutes. Stir in the mushrooms, herbs and salt and pepper, and cook for a further 5 minutes. Remove from the heat and stir in the tomatoes, tomato purée and the basil paste, if used.

Drain the rice, if necessary, and stir it into the tomato mixture. Use to fill the green peppers and place them close together in a well-greased ovenproof dish. Sprinkle with the grated cheese, cover and cook in a preheated oven for 15 minutes. Uncover and cook for a further 10–15 minutes, to allow the cheese to brown.

Variation:
Add any cooked meat, diced, when frying the nuts.

Watercress soufflé

Preparation time: 15–20 minutes
Cooking time: 30–35 minutes
Oven: 200°C, 400°F, Gas Mark 6

Metric	Imperial
40 g butter	1½ oz butter
100 g watercress, stalks removed, chopped	4 oz watercress, stalks removed, chopped
25 g plain wholemeal flour	1 oz plain wholemeal flour
300 ml milk	½ pint milk
1 × 1.25 ml spoon sea salt	¼ teaspoon sea salt
1 × 1.25 ml spoon paprika	¼ teaspoon paprika
1 × 1.25 ml spoon cayenne pepper	¼ teaspoon cayenne pepper
3 eggs (size 1 or 2), separated	3 eggs (size 1 or 2), separated
50 g Cheddar cheese, grated	2 oz Cheddar cheese, grated
1 egg white (size 1 or 2)	1 egg white (size 1 or 2)
25 g Parmesan cheese, grated	1 oz Parmesan cheese, grated

Melt 15 g/½ oz of the butter in a pan and add the watercress. Cover tightly and cook over a very low heat for 3–4 minutes.

Meanwhile, melt the rest of the butter in a large saucepan, stir in the flour and cook for 2 minutes. Gradually stir in the milk and bring to the boil. Simmer until thickened. Add the salt, paprika and cayenne pepper and remove from the heat. Beat in the egg yolks, one at a time. Stir in the Cheddar cheese and the softened watercress.

In a large bowl, beat the 4 egg whites until stiff enough to hold their shape. Stir one spoonful of the egg whites into the watercress mixture, then fold in the rest. Turn into a lightly greased 15 cm/6 inch soufflé dish, and sprinkle with the Parmesan cheese.

Cook in a preheated oven for 20–25 minutes or until the soufflé has risen and is lightly browned. Serve with Wholemeal Bread or Rolls (page 12).

Wholemeal vegetable samosas

Preparation time: 25 minutes
Cooking time: 40 minutes
Oven: 200°C, 400°F, Gas Mark 6

Metric
3 carrots, peeled and
  diced
4 medium potatoes,
  peeled and diced
1 × 2.5 ml spoon sea salt
1 × 2.5 ml spoon ground
  cumin
1 × 2.5 ml spoon ground
  coriander
1 × 5 ml spoon ground
  turmeric
1 × 1.25 ml spoon chilli
  powder
about 120 ml boiling
  water
5–6 spinach leaves, finely
  chopped

Pastry:
350 g self-raising
  wholemeal flour
1 × 2.5 ml spoon fine sea
  salt
75 g vegetable margarine
about 200 ml cold water
a little milk

Imperial
3 carrots, peeled and
  diced
4 medium potatoes,
  peeled and diced
½ teaspoon sea salt
½ teaspoon ground
  cumin
½ teaspoon ground
  coriander
1 teaspoon ground
  turmeric
¼ teaspoon chilli
  powder
about 4 fl oz boiling
  water
5–6 spinach leaves, finely
  chopped

Pastry:
12 oz self-raising
  wholemeal flour
½ teaspoon fine sea
  salt
3 oz vegetable margarine
about ⅓ pint cold water
a little milk

These samosas are baked, rather than deep-fried. Serve them as a snack, or for a light supper with a salad, or as a starter before a spicy main course such as Tandoori-Style Kebabs (page 40).

Put the carrots and potatoes into a saucepan with the salt, spices and boiling water. Cover tightly and simmer for 10 minutes. Shake the pan occasionally to prevent the vegetables sticking.
Add the spinach leaves and simmer for a further 5 minutes, adding a little more boiling water if necessary.
Meanwhile, make the pastry. Sift the flour and salt into a large mixing bowl, tipping in any bran left in the sieve. Rub in the margarine until the mixture resembles fine crumbs. Stir in enough water to make a soft dough, then shape the dough into a ball and divide into three portions.
Place one-third of the dough on to a floured board and roll out into a rectangle about 18 × 23 cm/7 × 9 inches. Spread one-third of the vegetable mixture along the length of the rectangle. Bring the long edges together, moistening each edge with a little milk to make them stick. Dust with a little flour and cut into the rectangle to make three squares. Repeat with the remaining dough and vegetable mixture.
Place the samosas on a greased and floured baking sheet. Cook in a preheated oven for 25 minutes.
Serve hot with an accompanying salad, such as Spicy Cauliflower Salad (page 57).
Makes 9

Wholemeal vegetable samosas;
Tomato and anchovy pizza

Tomato and anchovy pizza

Metric
15 g fresh yeast or 2 × 5
  ml spoons dried yeast
1 × 1.25 ml spoon
  Barbados sugar
150 ml warm water
225 g plain wheatmeal
  flour
1 × 5 ml spoon sea salt
2 × 5 ml spoons sunflower
  oil

Topping:
8 tomatoes, skinned and
  sliced, or 1 × 400 g can
  tomatoes, drained
175 g Mozzarella,
  Cheddar or Gruyère
  cheese, thinly sliced
1 × 50 g can anchovy
  fillets, drained
12 black olives, stoned
2 × 5 ml spoons dried
  oregano or basil
sea salt
freshly ground black
  pepper
2 × 15 ml spoons
  sunflower or olive oil

Imperial
½ oz fresh yeast or 2
  teaspoons dried yeast
¼ teaspoon Barbados
  sugar
¼ pint warm water
8 oz plain wheatmeal
  flour
1 teaspoon sea salt
2 teaspoons sunflower
  oil

Topping:
8 tomatoes, skinned and
  sliced, or 1 × 14 oz can
  tomatoes, drained
6 oz Mozzarella,
  Cheddar or Gruyère
  cheese, thinly sliced
1 × 2 oz can anchovy
  fillets, drained
12 black olives, stoned
2 teaspoons dried oregano
  or basil
sea salt
freshly ground black
  pepper
2 tablespoons sunflower
  or olive oil

Preparation time: 30 minutes, plus 30–60 minutes for
the dough to rise
Cooking time: 20–30 minutes
Oven: 220°C, 425°F, Gas Mark 7

If the kitchen is fairly warm the oven need not be
used, but in cooler surroundings it speeds up the
various processes to put the ingredients and dough in
a cool oven, as suggested in this recipe.

Cream the fresh yeast with the sugar and 5 × 15 ml
spoons/5 tablespoons of the warm water. (If using
dried yeast, dissolve the sugar in all of the water, then
stir in the dried yeast.) Place the yeast mixture in the
oven turned on to its lowest setting. Fresh yeast
should take 8–10 minutes to activate, dried yeast
about 5 minutes longer. The yeast is ready when it is
bubbling and frothy – if it has not started to bubble
after 15 minutes, it is too stale and should be
discarded. Sift the flour and salt into a large mixing
bowl and warm this in the oven too.
When the yeast is ready, remove both bowls from the
oven. Make a well in the centre of the dry ingredients
and pour in the oil, yeast mixture and any remaining
warm water. Mix to a stiff dough and form into a ball.
Put the dough on a lightly floured board, and return
the empty mixing bowl to the oven to keep it warm.
Knead the dough for 5–10 minutes, pushing the
dough away from you with the palms of your hands,
and then drawing it towards you with your fingertips,
folding the dough over as you pull it back. Keep
turning the dough as it is kneaded. When the dough
feels elastic and less sticky, roll it into a ball and put it
back in the warm mixing bowl. Cover with a clean
cloth, turn the oven off and leave the dough to rise in
the warmth of the switched-off oven for 30–60
minutes, or until it has nearly doubled in size.
Turn out the dough on to the floured board and knead
for a further 5 minutes. Roll it out into a large round,
or four smaller ones, about 5 mm/¼ inch thick. With a
rolling pin, lift the dough and place it on an oiled
baking sheet that allows room for the pizza to expand
in cooking.
To make the topping, spread the tomatoes over the
dough, leaving 5 mm/¼ inch around the edge so that
the filling does not run off the dough. Arrange the
cheese, anchovy fillets and olives on top. Sprinkle
with the oregano or basil and salt and pepper. Pour
over the oil.
Cook the pizza in a preheated oven for 20–30 minutes
or until the pastry base is crisp, and the cheese is
lightly browned. Serve hot with a green salad.
Makes one 30 cm/12 inch pizza or four 13 cm/5 inch
pizzas

Variation:
Substitute 2 × 5 ml spoons/2 teaspoons Pesto (page 31)
for the herbs.

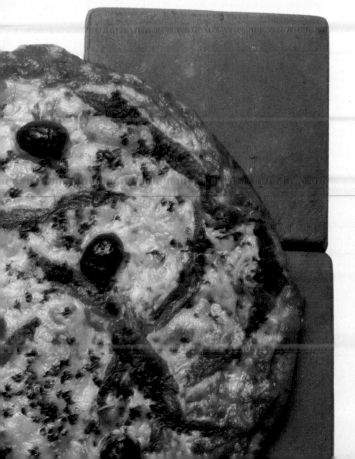

PASTA AND PULSES

A variety of types of wholemeal pasta are available from health food shops, delicatessens and some of the larger supermarkets. They contain five times as much dietary fibre as ordinary pasta, as well as B vitamins, vitamin E, essential minerals and a good deal of protein. Allow 75–100 g/3–4 oz pasta per person and follow the manufacturer's instructions for cooking.

Many dried beans, peas and lentils are also available from health food shops, delicatessens, oriental grocers and supermarkets. All pulses are high in protein, B vitamins and minerals, so they make an excellent alternative to meat, or a valuable ingredient to stretch meat dishes. Most pulses need to be soaked, the exception being whole or split lentils, before following the cooking instructions carefully.

Lentils are also the only dried pulse which may be salted while cooking. The others will not soften if salted in the early stages of cooking. Rinse pulses well before soaking, and pick them over to check that there are no stalks or small stones. Cold beans can be tossed into salads.

Tagliatelle with mushrooms and cream;
Spicy chick peas

Tagliatelle with mushrooms and cream

Metric	Imperial
350 g spinach tagliatelle	12 oz spinach tagliatelle
25 g butter	1 oz butter
225 g button mushrooms, thinly sliced	8 oz button mushrooms, thinly sliced
1 garlic clove, peeled and finely chopped (optional)	1 garlic clove, peeled and finely chopped (optional)
1 × 5 ml spoon dried oregano	1 teaspoon dried oregano
sea salt	sea salt
freshly ground black pepper	freshly ground black pepper
4 × 15 ml spoons single cream	4 tablespoons single cream

Preparation time: 5 minutes
Cooking time: 15–30 minutes

Spinach tagliatelle is not made from wholemeal flour, but it does make a delicious change now and again. For this recipe any pasta may be used.

Cook the pasta in boiling water, to which a few drops of oil have been added, until just tender.
Meanwhile, melt the butter in a frying pan and add the mushrooms with the garlic, if used, oregano and salt and pepper. Cover tightly and cook gently until the pasta is ready.
Drain the pasta and divide between individual warmed serving dishes. Top with the mushroom mixture and spoon a little cream over each serving. Sprinkle a little more pepper over each helping, and serve.

Variations:

Fry 50 g/2 oz bacon or cooked ham, cut into strips, with the mushrooms.
Add 225 g/8 oz freshly cooked, drained peas to the pasta with the mushrooms.

Spicy chick peas

Metric	Imperial
350 g dried chick peas, soaked overnight	12 oz dried chick peas, soaked overnight
3 × 15 ml spoons olive oil	3 tablespoons olive oil
2 large onions, peeled and chopped	2 large onions, peeled and chopped
2 garlic cloves, peeled and finely chopped	2 garlic cloves, peeled and finely chopped
2.5 cm fresh ginger root, peeled and finely chopped, or 1 × 5 ml spoon ground ginger	1 inch fresh ginger root, peeled and finely chopped, or 1 teaspoon ground ginger
1 × 5 ml spoon ground turmeric	1 teaspoon ground turmeric
1 × 5 ml spoon ground cardamom or 4 whole green cardamoms	1 teaspoon ground cardamom or 4 whole green cardamoms
2 green peppers, cored, seeded and chopped	2 green peppers, cored, seeded and chopped
2 × 5 ml spoons ground cumin	2 teaspoons ground cumin
1 × 2.5 ml spoon chilli powder (more or less, to taste)	½ teaspoon chilli powder (more or less, to taste)
1 × 5 ml spoon tomato purée	1 teaspoon tomato purée
450 g potatoes, boiled in their skins and cubed	1 lb potatoes, boiled in their skins and cubed
sea salt	sea salt
freshly ground black pepper	freshly ground black pepper
chopped fresh parsley, to garnish	chopped fresh parsley, to garnish

Preparation time: 15 minutes, plus overnight soaking
Cooking time: 1½–2½ hours

Drain the chick peas and put them into a saucepan. Cover with fresh cold water and bring to the boil, then boil for 10 minutes. Cover and simmer for 1–2 hours or until tender. Drain.
Heat the oil in a large, deep saucepan, add the onion and fry until browned. Add the garlic, ginger, turmeric and cardamom. Fry gently, stirring, for 2–3 minutes. Add the peppers and fry for 5 minutes.
Add the chick peas and fry for a further 10 minutes, stirring occasionally and adding more oil if necessary. Stir in the cumin, chilli powder and tomato purée, then add the potatoes with salt and pepper. Cook just long enough for the potatoes to heat through, without becoming mushy. The dish should have a glossy sauce and not be too dry.
Sprinkle with a little parsley and serve, topped with a spoonful of Natural Yogurt (page 8), hand round a bowl of Yogurt Sauce (page 40) separately.

Simple garlic sauce; Fresh tomato sauce; Pesto; Bolognese sauce

Simple garlic sauce

Metric
3 × 15 ml spoons olive oil
  or 40 g butter
1 small onion, peeled and
  finely chopped
1–2 garlic cloves, peeled
  and finely chopped
sea salt
freshly ground black
  pepper
chopped fresh parsley

Imperial
3 tablespoons olive oil or
  1½ oz butter
1 small onion, peeled and
  finely chopped
1–2 garlic cloves, peeled
  and finely chopped
sea salt
freshly ground black
  pepper
chopped fresh parsley

Preparation time: 5–10 minutes
Cooking time: 5 minutes

This is an inexpensive and good sauce to serve with wholemeal pasta, in particular, spaghetti. Use butter unless you have really first-class olive oil.

Heat the oil or melt the butter in a small saucepan, add the onion and garlic and fry until transparent. Pour over freshly cooked, drained pasta. Add salt and lots of pepper, sprinkle generously with parsley and serve. Hand round a dish of grated Cheddar or Parmesan cheese separately.

Fresh tomato sauce

Metric
1 kg ripe tomatoes,
  chopped
1 onion, peeled and finely
  chopped
1 carrot, scraped and
  finely chopped
1 celery stick, finely
  chopped
1 small leek, chopped
1 × 2.5 ml spoon sea salt
1 × 1.25 ml spoon
  demerara sugar
1 × 2.5 ml spoon dried
  oregano
1 × 2.5 ml spoon dried
  basil
1 × 15 ml spoon tomato
  purée
freshly ground black
  pepper

Imperial
2 lb ripe tomatoes,
  chopped
1 onion, peeled and finely
  chopped
1 carrot, scraped and
  finely chopped
1 celery stick, finely
  chopped
1 small leek, chopped
½ teaspoon sea salt
¼ teaspoon demerara
  sugar
½ teaspoon dried
  oregano
½ teaspoon dried
  basil
1 tablespoon tomato
  purée
freshly ground black
  pepper

Preparation time: 15 minutes
Cooking time: 50 minutes

This is a good sauce to make when tomatoes are cheap. You may substitute canned tomatoes, but remember they may have salt and sugar already added. This sauce makes the perfect accompaniment to many meat dishes, such as Hamburgers (page 41), and fish and vegetables, as well as to all kinds of pasta. It is worth making the full amount and storing any left over in the refrigerator to be used later in the week. This sauce also freezes well.

Put all the ingredients into a saucepan and bring to the boil. Stir, then cover tightly and simmer for 40–45 minutes.
Strain into a clean saucepan, pressing all the juice out of the mixture with the back of a spoon. Boil, uncovered, for a few minutes to thicken the sauce, then taste and adjust the seasoning.
To serve four, cook 450 g/1 lb wholemeal spaghetti and pour 300 ml/½ pint tomato sauce over. Sprinkle with parsley and serve with grated Parmesan cheese.
Makes about 600 ml/1 pint

Bolognese sauce

Metric	Imperial
1 × 15 ml spoon olive oil or 15 g butter	1 tablespoon olive oil or ½ oz butter
1 onion, peeled and chopped	1 onion, peeled and chopped
350–450 g lean minced beef	12 oz–1 lb lean minced beef
2 garlic cloves, peeled and chopped	2 garlic cloves, peeled and chopped
6 tomatoes, peeled and chopped, or 1 × 400 g can tomatoes (optional)	6 tomatoes, peeled and chopped, or 1 × 14 oz can tomatoes (optional)
120 ml red wine	4 fl oz red wine
2 × 15 ml spoons water or Stock (page 16)	2 tablespoons water or Stock (page 16)
1 bay leaf	1 bay leaf
1 × 1.25 ml spoon ground cinnamon	¼ teaspoon ground cinnamon
pinch of grated nutmeg	pinch of grated nutmeg
1 × 2.5 ml spoon dried oregano	½ teaspoon dried oregano
2 × 15 ml spoons tomato purée	2 tablespoons tomato purée
sea salt	sea salt
freshly ground black pepper	freshly ground black pepper

Preparation time: 10 minutes
Cooking time: 35–50 minutes

This is a delicious, rich sauce with a slightly sweet flavour from the cinnamon.

Heat the oil or melt the butter in a saucepan, add the onion and fry until transparent. Add the beef and garlic and continue frying until the meat is lightly browned. Stir in the tomatoes, if used, the wine and stock or water and add the bay leaf, cinnamon, nutmeg, oregano, tomato purée and salt and pepper. Bring to the boil, then cover tightly and simmer for 30–40 minutes until the meat is cooked.
Uncover the pan and cook for a further 5–10 minutes to thicken the sauce. Taste and adjust the seasoning and discard the bay leaf before serving, with any kind of wholemeal pasta.

Pesto

Metric	Imperial
75 g fresh basil leaves, chopped, or 25 g dried basil with 9–10 × 15 ml spoons boiled water, cooled	3 oz fresh basil leaves, chopped, or 1 oz dried basil with 9–10 tablespoons boiled water, cooled
50 g pine nuts	2 oz pine nuts
2–3 garlic cloves, peeled and chopped	2–3 garlic cloves, peeled and chopped
1 × 2.5 ml spoon fine sea salt	½ teaspoon fine sea salt
120 ml olive or sunflower oil	4 fl oz olive or sunflower oil
50 g Parmesan cheese, grated	2 oz Parmesan cheese, grated

Preparation time: 10–15 minutes

This is worth making in fairly large quantities, as it keeps very well in the refrigerator. A little pesto lends a special flavour to Tomato and Anchovy Pizza (page 27). Use it in Stuffed Green Peppers (page 25) or in baked jacket potatoes with an equal quantity of butter. The traditional Genoese way of serving pasta is to stir 2–3 × 15 ml spoons/2–3 tablespoons pesto and 15 g/½ oz butter into enough cooked pasta for four in the warmed serving bowl. Cashew nuts or walnuts may be substituted for the pine nuts.

If using dried basil, mix it with the water and leave to soak until the water has been absorbed. No water is needed if using fresh basil.
Put the pine nuts into a blender goblet with the fresh or soaked dried basil, garlic, salt and 1 × 15 ml spoon/1 tablespoon of the oil. Blend together, then add the Parmesan cheese and gradually pour in the oil, blending all the time, like making mayonnaise. If you haven't got a blender, pound the ingredients with a pestle and mortar. When all the oil has been incorporated, the paste should be quite solid.
Store in a screw-top jar, sealed with a layer of oil or melted butter, and use as required.
Makes about 350 ml/12 fl oz

Wholemeal lasagne

Metric	Imperial
225 g wholemeal lasagne	*8 oz wholemeal lasagne*
Bolognese Sauce, made with 450 g beef and tomatoes (page 31)	*Bolognese Sauce, made with 1 lb beef and tomatoes (page 31)*
225 g ricotta, curd or sieved cottage cheese	*8 oz ricotta, curd or sieved cottage cheese*
50 g Parmesan cheese	*2 oz Parmesan cheese*
25 g butter	*1 oz butter*
2 × 15 ml spoons plain wholemeal flour	*2 tablespoons plain wholemeal flour*
300 ml hot milk	*¼ pint hot milk*
sea salt	*sea salt*
freshly ground black pepper	*freshly ground black pepper*
pinch of grated nutmeg	*pinch of grated nutmeg*
1 egg yolk, beaten	*1 egg yolk, beaten*

Preparation time: 45 minutes
Cooking time: 35–40 minutes
Oven: 180°C, 350°F, Gas Mark 4

Cook the lasagne in boiling water, to which a few drops of oil have been added, for 10–20 minutes or until just tender. Drain on a clean tea towel.
Spread one-quarter of the bolognese sauce over the bottom of a greased deep ovenproof dish. Cover with one-third of the lasagne, then one-third of the soft cheese. Sprinkle with 1 × 5 ml spoon/1 teaspoon of the Parmesan cheese. Repeat the layers twice, then spoon over the remaining bolognese sauce. To make the white sauce, melt the butter in a pan, stir in the flour and cook for 2 minutes. Stir in the milk and simmer until thickened. Add salt, pepper and nutmeg to taste. Stir a spoonful of the sauce into the egg yolk. Stir this mixture into the remaining sauce, then pour it over the bolognese sauce. Sprinkle over the remaining Parmesan cheese. Cook in a preheated oven for 30–35 minutes until lightly browned and hot.
Serves 6

Wholemeal macaroni carbonara

Metric	Imperial
350–450 g wholemeal macaroni	*12–16 oz wholemeal macaroni*
15 g butter	*½ oz butter*
175 g cooked ham or green bacon, cut into short thin strips	*6 oz cooked ham or green bacon, cut into short thin strips*
sea salt	*sea salt*
freshly ground black pepper	*freshly ground black pepper*
2 × 15 ml spoons cream	*2 tablespoons cream*
3 eggs, beaten	*3 eggs, beaten*
about 50 g Parmesan cheese, grated	*about 2 oz Parmesan cheese, grated*

Preparation time: 5 minutes
Cooking time: 10–20 minutes

Use wholemeal spaghetti if you haven't any wholemeal macaroni.

Cook the macaroni in boiling water, to which a few drops of oil have been added, for 10–20 minutes or until just tender.
Meanwhile, melt the butter in a large pan, add the ham or bacon and fry gently until it is fairly crisp. Add a little salt, depending upon how salty the meat is, and lots of pepper.
In a bowl beat the cream with the eggs.
Drain the macaroni and stir into the ham or bacon. Turn off the heat and add the cream and eggs, stirring constantly. The eggs will cook and thicken slightly from the warmth of the pasta. Serve at once on hot plates and sprinkle with Parmesan cheese. A tomato salad makes a good accompaniment.

Pasta with ricotta cheese

Preparation time: 5 minutes
Cooking time: 10–20 minutes

Metric
350 g pasta
25 g butter
225 g curd or ricotta
  cheese, roughly chopped
pinch of grated nutmeg
1 garlic clove, peeled and
  crushed (optional)
sea salt
freshly ground black
  pepper
2 × 15 ml spoons chopped
  fresh parsley
50 g Parmesan cheese,
  grated, to serve

Imperial
12 oz pasta
1 oz butter
8 oz curd or ricotta
  cheese, roughly chopped
pinch of grated nutmeg
1 garlic clove, peeled and
  crushed (optional)
sea salt
freshly ground black
  pepper
2 tablespoons chopped
  fresh parsley
2 oz Parmesan cheese,
  grated, to serve

This dish is delicious served on its own or it makes a good accompaniment to grilled meat or Herbed Skinless Sausages (page 10).

Cook the pasta in boiling water, to which a few drops of oil have been added, until just tender. Drain well and transfer to a warmed serving dish. Add the butter, ricotta or curd cheese, nutmeg, garlic, if used, and salt and pepper to taste. Mix well, then toss with the parsley and serve. Hand round a bowl of grated cheese separately.

Wholemeal lasagne; Wholemeal macaroni carbonara;
Pasta with ricotta cheese

Brown rice with almonds

Preparation time: 10–15 minutes
Cooking time: about 55 minutes

Metric

2 × 15 ml spoons olive oil
25 g flaked almonds or
  sunflower seeds
1 large onion, peeled and
  chopped
1 × 5 ml spoon cumin
  seeds
225 g long-grain brown
  rice
pinch of nutmeg, allspice
  or a little freshly
  ground black pepper
600 ml hot Stock (page
  16) or water
1 × 15 ml spoon fresh
  marigold petals or
  1½ × 5 ml spoons dried
  marigold petals
  (optional)
1 bay leaf
1 × 2.5 cm cinnamon stick
  or 1 × 5 ml spoon
  ground cinnamon
about 1 × 5 ml spoon sea
  salt

Imperial

2 tablespoons olive oil
1 oz flaked almonds or
  sunflower seeds
1 large onion, peeled and
  chopped
1 teaspoon cumin
  seeds
8 oz long-grain brown
  rice
pinch of nutmeg, allspice
  or a little freshly
  ground black pepper
1 pint hot Stock (page
  16) or water
1 tablespoon fresh
  marigold petals or 1½
  teaspoons dried
  marigold petals
  (optional)
1 bay leaf
1 × 1 inch cinnamon stick
  or 1 teaspoon ground
  cinnamon
about 1 teaspoon sea
  salt

Brown rice with almonds; Hearty lentil casserole

This is a lovely accompaniment to all pulse dishes, as well as to spicy dishes generally. It's also very good on its own, sprinkled with freshly ground black pepper and chopped fresh parsley, served with a salad or a few braised vegetables. If you prefer, cook the rice in a preheated oven, at 160°C, 325°F, Gas Mark 3. Bring to the boil on top of the stove first. Dried marigold petals are available from health food shops.

Heat the oil in a deep frying pan, add the almonds or sunflower seeds and fry gently until lightly browned. Remove the nuts or seeds and set on one side.
Add the onion to the pan and fry in the hot oil until well browned. Stir in the cumin, rice, nutmeg, allspice or pepper, and fry, stirring, for 1–2 minutes. Add the hot stock or water, marigold petals, bay leaf, cinnamon and salt to taste. Bring to the boil and stir once, cover tightly and simmer for 35–40 minutes. Uncover the pan, add the almonds or sunflower seeds and continue to cook for 5 minutes without a lid, until all the liquid has been absorbed. The rice should be cooked but still chewy. Alternatively, if more convenient, remove the pan from the heat and leave in a warm place, covered, for 10 minutes. Taste and adjust the seasoning, and discard the bay leaf, before serving.

Variations:

Boiled brown rice: put 225 g/8 oz long-grain brown rice and 600 ml/1 pint stock or water in a saucepan with 1 × 5 ml spoon/1 teaspoon sea salt (less salt if the stock is salted). Bring to the boil, then cover and simmer for 35–40 minutes. Remove the lid and simmer until all the moisture is absorbed.
Brown rice with onion: follow the recipe for Brown Rice with Almonds, omitting the almonds or sunflower seeds, marigold petals, cumin and cinnamon. Use only 1 × 15 ml spoon/1 tablespoon of olive oil.

Hearty lentil casserole

Preparation time: 20 minutes, plus soaking time
Cooking time: about 1¼ hours

Metric
1 aubergine, chopped
sea salt
2 × 15 ml spoons olive oil
1 onion, peeled and
  chopped
1 garlic clove, peeled and
  chopped
4 carrots, scraped and
  chopped
2 celery sticks, chopped
2 parsnips, peeled and cut
  into 2.5 cm strips
225 g whole green or
  brown lentils, rinsed
900 ml hot Stock (page
  16) or water
1 bay leaf
1 parsley sprig
1 × 5 ml spoon dried
  savory
1 × 5 ml spoon dried
  marjoram
1 × 5 ml spoon tomato
  purée
freshly ground black
  pepper
225 g courgettes, thickly
  sliced
450 g pork sausages
chopped fresh parsley, to
  garnish

Imperial
1 aubergine, chopped
sea salt
2 tablespoons olive oil
1 onion, peeled and
  chopped
1 garlic clove, peeled and
  chopped
4 carrots, scraped and
  chopped
2 celery sticks, chopped
2 parsnips, peeled and cut
  into 1 inch strips
8 oz whole green or brown
  lentils, rinsed
1½ pints hot Stock (page
  16) or water
1 bay leaf
1 parsley sprig
1 teaspoon dried
  savory
1 teaspoon dried
  marjoram
1 teaspoon tomato
  purée
freshly ground black
  pepper
8 oz courgettes, thickly
  sliced
1 lb pork sausages
chopped fresh parsley, to
  garnish

Put the aubergine into a colander. Sprinkle with salt and cover with a plate, weighted down. Leave for at least 30 minutes. Rinse the aubergine in cold water and drain on paper towels.

Heat the oil in a large, deep saucepan, add the onion and fry until transparent. Add the garlic and aubergine and fry for 5 minutes more. Stir in the carrots, celery, parsnips and lentils and pour over the hot stock or water. Bring to the boil, then boil for 10 minutes, skimming if necessary.

Add the bay leaf, parsley, savory, marjoram, tomato purée and salt and pepper. Cover tightly and simmer very gently for 35 minutes, stirring occasionally to make sure that the lentils do not stick to the bottom of the pan.

Add the courgettes, with a little more hot stock or water if there isn't enough liquid in the pan. Cover tightly again and simmer gently for a further 15 minutes or until the courgettes are tender and the liquid has been absorbed. Should there be too much liquid, cook uncovered for a few minutes.

Meanwhile, grill the sausages, then slice them thickly.

Taste and adjust the seasoning, and discard the bay leaf, then transfer the vegetable mixture to a warmed serving dish. Stir in the sausages, sprinkle with parsley and serve with a green salad.

Variation:
A substantial vegetarian dish may be made by replacing the sausages with cauliflower. Trim off the stalk of the cauliflower and cut into small florets. Add with the courgettes.

Spiced red beans

Preparation time: 15 minutes, plus soaking time
Cooking time: 1¾–2¾ hours

Metric
350 g dried red kidney or
rose cocoa beans,
soaked for at least 2
hours or overnight
2 × 15 ml spoons oil
1 large onion, peeled and
chopped
225 g mushrooms,
chopped
25 g creamed coconut, cut
into small pieces
juice of 1 lemon
sea salt
freshly ground black
pepper
chopped fresh coriander
leaves or parsley, to
garnish

Sauce:
1 × 5 ml spoon ground
cumin
1 × 2.5 ml spoon ground
ginger
1 × 5 ml spoon ground
coriander
1 × 5 ml spoon ground
cardamom
1 × 15 ml spoon single
cream
4 × 15 ml spoons Natural
Yogurt (page 8)
1 × 5 ml spoon tomato
purée
1 × 15 ml spoon
desiccated coconut or
grated fresh coconut
pinch of grated nutmeg

Imperial
12 oz dried red kidney or
rose cocoa beans,
soaked for at least 2
hours or overnight
2 tablespoons oil
1 large onion, peeled and
chopped
8 oz mushrooms,
chopped
1 oz creamed coconut, cut
into small pieces
juice of 1 lemon
sea salt
freshly ground black
pepper
chopped fresh coriander
leaves or parsley, to
garnish

Sauce:
1 teaspoon ground
cumin
½ teaspoon ground
ginger
1 teaspoon ground
coriander
1 teaspoon ground
cardamom
1 tablespoon single
cream
4 tablespoons Natural
Yogurt (page 8)
1 teaspoon tomato
purée
1 tablespoon desiccated
coconut or grated fresh
coconut
pinch of grated nutmeg

This delicately spiced dish is very quick to prepare once the beans are cooked, although canned beans may be substituted. Creamed coconut is available from some supermarkets.

Put the beans and their soaking water into a large saucepan. Bring to the boil, boil for 10 minutes, then cover and simmer gently for 1–2 hours or until soft. Top up the water when necessary. Drain.
Heat the oil in another large saucepan, add the onion and fry until browned. Add the mushrooms and cook gently for a further 5 minutes, then stir in the beans. Combine all the sauce ingredients in a bowl or blender and stir thoroughly or blend until smooth. Pour over the beans and vegetables. Add the creamed coconut and continue to cook gently, stirring, until the creamed coconut has melted.
Pour the lemon juice over, add salt and pepper to taste, and cook for a further 5–10 minutes, stirring constantly. Serve very hot, sprinkled with chopped coriander leaves or parsley.

Black-eye pea casserole

Preparation time: 15 minutes, plus soaking time
Cooking time: 2 hours 10 minutes
Oven: 180°C, 350°F, Gas Mark 4

Metric	Imperial
225 g dried black-eye peas, soaked for at least 1 hour	8 oz dried black-eye peas, soaked for at least 1 hour
3 × 15 ml spoons olive oil	3 tablespoons olive oil
1 large onion, peeled and chopped	1 large onion, peeled and chopped
2 garlic cloves, peeled and chopped	2 garlic cloves, peeled and chopped
2 potatoes, peeled and sliced	2 potatoes, peeled and sliced
2 large carrots, scraped and chopped	2 large carrots, scraped and chopped
2 turnips, peeled and diced	2 turnips, peeled and diced
2 parsnips, peeled and diced	2 parsnips, peeled and diced
2 celery sticks, chopped	2 celery sticks, chopped
1 × 15 ml spoon chopped fresh parsley	1 tablespoon chopped fresh parsley
1 × 5 ml spoon dried thyme	1 tablespoon dried thyme
1 × 5 ml spoon dried oregano	1 teaspoon dried oregano
2 bay leaves	2 bay leaves
sea salt	sea salt
freshly ground black pepper	freshly ground black pepper
1 × 5 ml spoon black treacle	1 teaspoon black treacle
2 × 15 ml spoons tomato purée	2 tablespoons tomato purée
50 g Cheddar cheese, grated (optional)	2 oz Cheddar cheese, grated (optional)

Put the black-eye peas and their soaking water into a large saucepan. Bring to the boil, boil for 10 minutes, then cover and simmer gently for 20 minutes.

Meanwhile, heat the oil in a flameproof casserole, add the onion and garlic and fry until transparent. Stir in the potatoes, carrots, turnips, parsnips and celery. Cover tightly and cook over a gentle heat for 10 minutes, stirring occasionally to prevent the vegetables sticking to the pan.

Drain the black-eye peas, which should be almost tender, reserving their cooking liquid. Stir the drained peas into the casserole with the herbs and salt and pepper. Pour over 600 ml/1 pint of the reserved cooking liquid, adding more if necessary so that all the vegetables and peas are covered.

Stir in the black treacle and tomato purée. Cover tightly and transfer to a preheated oven. Cook for 1½ hours.

Uncover the casserole and discard the bay leaves. Sprinkle with the grated cheese, if used. Cook without a lid for a further 10 minutes. This allows the juices in the pan to evaporate and thicken slightly, and for the cheese to melt.

Variation:

Substitute dried butter beans for the black-eye peas, but they must be soaked overnight and then cooked in their soaking water, with extra water if necessary for 2½ hours, before adding them to the vegetables.

Spiced red beans; Black-eye pea casserole

MEAT, POULTRY AND FISH

Meat, poultry and fish are all excellent sources of protein. Meat is rich in iron and in B vitamins; the latter help the body to make full use of nutrients. Buy the best produce you can afford, rather than eating cheap, fatty cuts, and eat poultry or fish in preference to red meat each day. Eating large quantities of protein-rich foods beyond the amount the body requires does not particularly improve your health. When you prepare meat, cut away as much visible fat as possible, and grill or casserole the meat rather than fry it. If you have a mincer, mince your own beef from chuck or stewing steak, of if you can afford it grilling steak, so that you can be sure that it will be lean.

Fish and poultry are both low in fat and are very useful as a basis around which to prepare a meal. Buy and eat fish while it is as fresh as possible.

Spare ribs with ginger; Pork with parsnip and apple

Pork with parsnip and apple

Metric
3–4 × 15 ml spoons olive oil
450 g pork fillet, cubed
1 large onion, peeled and chopped
3 × 15 ml spoons plain wholemeal flour
2 medium parsnips, peeled and chopped
1 large cooking apple, peeled, cored and chopped
450 ml strong dry cider
1 × 2.5 ml spoon dry mustard
1 × 2.5 ml spoon dried thyme
2 × 5 ml spoons dried tarragon
1 × 2.5 ml spoon sea salt
4 drops Worcestershire sauce
1 parsley sprig
freshly ground black pepper

Imperial
3–4 tablespoons olive oil
1 lb pork fillet, cubed
1 large onion, peeled and chopped
3 tablespoons plain wholemeal flour
2 medium parsnips, peeled and chopped
1 large cooking apple, peeled, cored and chopped
¾ pint strong dry cider
½ teaspoon dry mustard
½ teaspoon dried thyme
2 teaspoons dried tarragon
½ teaspoon sea salt
4 drops Worcestershire sauce
1 parsley sprig
freshly ground black pepper

Preparation time: 15 minutes
Cooking time: 55 minutes
Oven: 180°C, 350°F, Gas Mark 4

Heat the oil in a flameproof casserole, add the pork and brown on all sides. Remove the pork from the casserole. Add the onion and fry until soft. Stir in the flour and cook for 1–2 minutes. Add the parsnip and fry for a further 2 minutes, stirring.

Return the pork to the casserole with the apple and pour over the cider. Bring to the boil, stirring until thickened. Add a little more cider or water if necessary. Stir in the remaining ingredients, cover tightly and transfer to a preheated oven. Cook for 45 minutes or until the meat is tender. Taste and adjust the seasoning.

Serve with a simple salad and potatoes thinly sliced and layered in an ovenproof dish, dotted with butter, well seasoned and baked in the oven on the shelf above the pork casserole.

Spare ribs with ginger

Metric
2 kg pork spare ribs, trimmed of excess fat and cut into single rib pieces

Sauce:
juice of 1 lemon
1 × 15 ml spoon clear honey
1 × 5 ml spoon paprika
3 × 15 ml spoons soy sauce
1 cm fresh ginger root, peeled and finely chopped, or 1 × 5 ml spoon ground ginger
2 garlic cloves, peeled and crushed
1 × 5 ml spoon dry or made mustard
1 × 15 ml spoon sherry (optional)
sea salt
freshly ground black pepper

Imperial
4 lb pork spare ribs, trimmed of excess fat and cut into single rib pieces

Sauce:
juice of 1 lemon
1 tablespoon clear honey
1 teaspoon paprika
3 tablespoons soy sauce
½ inch fresh ginger root, peeled and finely chopped, or 1 teaspoon ground ginger
2 garlic cloves, peeled and crushed
1 teaspoon dry or made mustard
1 tablespoon sherry (optional)
sea salt
freshly ground black pepper

Preparation time: 10 minutes
Cooking time: 1¼ hours
Oven: 200°C, 400°F, Gas Mark 6; 180°C, 350°F, Gas Mark 4

Ask your butcher to prepare the spare ribs for cooking Chinese-style. The best way to eat spare ribs is with your fingers, so it is a good idea to put out finger bowls with a slice of lemon in the water.

Put the spare ribs on a rack in a roasting tin and cook in a preheated oven for 30 minutes.

Meanwhile, prepare the sauce. Put all the sauce ingredients in a bowl, with salt and pepper to taste, and stir thoroughly.

Remove the spare ribs from the oven and reduce the oven temperature. Transfer the ribs to a plate. Remove the roasting rack and tip away all the fat from the tin. Put the ribs back into the tin, without the rack, and pour over the sauce. Return to the oven and cook for a further 45 minutes, turning the ribs frequently in the sauce. The ribs should be sweet, succulent and well glazed. Serve hot with a salad or vegetable such as Stir-fried Cabbage (page 68).

Tandoori-style spicy kebabs

Preparation time: 10–15 minutes
Cooking time: 15 minutes

Metric
450 g lean minced beef
1 garlic clove, peeled and crushed
2.5 cm fresh ginger root, peeled and chopped
1½ × 5 ml spoon paprika
1 × 15 ml spoon tandoori mixture
1 × 2.5 ml spoon ground coriander
pinch of chilli powder
1 × 2.5 ml spoon sea salt
freshly ground black pepper
1 egg, beaten
juice of ½ lemon

Yogurt sauce:
150 ml Natural Yogurt (page 8)
1 × 1.25 ml spoon fine sea salt
3–4 fresh mint leaves, chopped, or 1 × 5 ml spoon dried mint
1 × 1.25 ml spoon clear honey
1 garlic clove, peeled and crushed
1 × 5 ml spoon dried fenugreek leaves
1 × 2.5 ml spoon ground coriander or 1 × 5 ml spoon chopped fresh coriander leaves
freshly ground black pepper
1 × 15 ml spoon sunflower oil
pinch of chilli powder (optional)

To garnish:
few chopped fresh coriander leaves or parsley
lemon wedges

Imperial
1 lb lean minced beef
1 garlic clove, peeled and crushed
1 inch fresh ginger root, peeled and chopped
1½ teaspoons paprika
1 tablespoon tandoori mixture
½ teaspoon ground coriander
pinch of chilli powder
½ teaspoon sea salt
freshly ground black pepper
1 egg, beaten
juice of ½ lemon

Yogurt sauce:
¼ pint Natural Yogurt (page 8)
¼ teaspoon fine sea salt
3–4 fresh mint leaves, chopped, or 1 teaspoon dried mint
¼ teaspoon clear honey
1 garlic clove, peeled and crushed
1 teaspoon dried fenugreek leaves
½ teaspoon ground coriander or 1 teaspoon chopped fresh coriander leaves
freshly ground black pepper
1 tablespoon sunflower oil
pinch of chilli powder (optional)

To garnish:
few chopped fresh coriander leaves or parsley
lemon wedges

Fenugreek leaves and the tandoori mixture, which is a powder, are available from Asian shops and certain supermarkets. To turn the yogurt sauce into an accompaniment add half a cucumber, thinly peeled and grated.

Put the meat into a large mixing bowl. Add the garlic, ginger, 1 × 2.5 ml spoon/½ teaspoon of the paprika, the tandoori mixture, ground coriander, chilli powder, and salt and pepper. Mix well and work in the beaten egg. Set aside for 5 minutes. Mould the mixture into long, thin shapes on 4–6 greased skewers.

To make the yogurt sauce, mix all the ingredients in a bowl. Sprinkle with 1.25 ml spoon/½ teaspoon of the paprika from the kebab ingredients.

Cook the kebabs under a preheated grill for 15 minutes, turning them frequently, or until browned and cooked through. Sprinkle with the lemon juice and the rest of the paprika.

Garnish with coriander leaves or parsley and lemon wedges, and hand round a bowl of yogurt sauce separately. Serve as a starter, with a green salad, or as a main course accompanied by Brown Rice with Almonds (page 34).

Serves 4–6

Tandoori-style spicy kebabs; Hamburgers

Hamburgers

Preparation time: 10 minutes
Cooking time: 10–15 minutes

Metric	**Imperial**
450 g very lean minced beef	1 lb very lean minced beef
1 × 2.5 ml spoon dried savory	½ teaspoon dried savory
2 drops Worcestershire sauce	2 drops Worcestershire sauce
1 × 1.25 ml spoon dry mustard	½ teaspoon dry mustard
sea salt	sea salt
freshly ground black pepper	freshly ground black pepper
1 egg, beaten	1 egg, beaten
about 2 × 5 ml spoons plain wholemeal flour	about 2 teaspoons plain wholemeal flour

These should be made with the very best meat that you can afford. If you mince the meat yourself, buy grilling or frying steak if you can, or lean braising or stewing steak, and cut away all the visible fat.

These hamburgers can also be served inside a sesame bun accompanied with relishes.

Put the meat into a large mixing bowl with the savory, Worcestershire sauce, mustard, and salt and pepper. Mix well, then work in the egg. Add just enough flour to bind the mixture together.

Shape into four thin, flat rounds, using a hamburger mould if you have one. Cook under a preheated grill for about 5 minutes on each side or until well browned and cooked all the way through.

Serve with a salad, such as Spinach Salad (page 57), and baked jacket potatoes, split and filled with butter and chopped fresh parsley, or with soured cream and chopped fresh chives. Accompany with mustard and relishes or Fresh Tomato Sauce (page 30).

Pork chops with lemon and herbs

Preparation time: 10 minutes, plus marinating
Cooking time: about 15 minutes

This dish is speedily prepared but is best if the chops are marinated overnight.

Prepare the pork chops by cutting the fat at right-angles to the meat in several places, so that the meat does not curl in cooking.

Make one or two shallow cuts in the meat and insert one or two crushed juniper berries into each chop. Sprinkle with salt and pepper on both sides then put the chops in a dish, sprinkle with the herbs and pour over the lemon juice. Leave to marinate for 2 hours. When ready to cook, drain the chops and pat dry with paper towels. Brush with a little oil and cook under a preheated grill for about 15 minutes until thoroughly cooked. Turn the chops every few minutes.

Garnish with fresh herbs and a twist of lemon. Serve with Baked Red Cabbage (page 68) or Cabbage with Mustard Soured Cream Dressing (page 62).

Metric
4 thick pork chops
4–8 juniper berries,
  lightly crushed
sea salt
freshly ground black
  pepper
2 × 15 ml spoons chopped
fresh herbs e.g. parsley
or thyme or savory or
tarragon
juice of 2 lemons
1 × 15 ml spoon olive or
sunflower oil

To garnish:
chopped fresh parsley
4 twists of lemon

Imperial
4 thick pork chops
4–8 juniper berries,
  lightly crushed
sea salt
freshly ground black
  pepper
2 tablespoons chopped
fresh herbs e.g. parsley
or thyme or savory or
tarragon
juice of 2 lemons
1 tablespoon olive or
sunflower oil

To garnish:
chopped fresh herbs
4 twists of lemon

Stuffed shoulder of lamb;
Pork chops with lemon and herbs

42

Stuffed shoulder of lamb

Preparation time: 15 minutes
Cooking time: 2½ hours
Oven: 220°C, 425°F, Gas Mark 7;
180°C, 350°F, Gas Mark 4

Metric
1 × about 2 kg shoulder
of lamb, boned
juice of 1 large lemon
1 × 5 ml spoon dry
mustard
1 × 5 ml spoon demerara
sugar
finely grated rind of 1
lemon
juice of ½ orange
watercress, to garnish

Stuffing:
2 bunches watercress,
stalks removed,
chopped
1 × 5 ml spoon chopped
fresh rosemary or
1 × 2.5 ml spoon dried
rosemary
1 orange, peeled and
chopped
grated rind of ½ orange
1 onion, peeled and finely
chopped
1 garlic clove, peeled and
crushed
1 × 2.5 ml spoon sea salt
freshly ground black
pepper

Imperial
1 × about 4 lb shoulder of
lamb, boned
juice of 1 large lemon
1 teaspoon dry
mustard
1 teaspoon demerara
sugar
finely grated rind of 1
lemon
juice of ½ orange
watercress, to garnish

Stuffing:
2 bunches watercress,
stalks removed,
chopped
1 teaspoon chopped
fresh rosemary or
½ teaspoon dried
rosemary
1 orange, peeled and
chopped
grated rind of ½ orange
1 onion, peeled and finely
chopped
1 garlic clove, peeled and
crushed
½ teaspoon sea salt
freshly ground black
pepper

The lemon and orange flavour freshens this rather fatty cut of meat. Try to buy the new season lamb, either New Zealand or English, which is leaner than older meat.

Trim off as much excess fat from the meat as possible, then lay the meat on a flat surface, skin side down. Combine all the ingredients for the stuffing in a bowl, then spread over the meat. Roll up the lamb and secure with string at 2.5 cm/1 inch intervals.

Place the lamb on a rack in a roasting tin. Pour over half of the lemon juice. Mix 1 × 2.5 ml spoon/½ teaspoon of the mustard with 1 × 2.5 ml spoon/½ teaspoon of the sugar and all the lemon rind, and rub this over the meat. Roast in a preheated oven for 15 minutes to seal the meat, then reduce the oven temperature and continue to roast for 30 minutes to each 450 g/1 lb of the original boned meat weight. Transfer the meat to a warmed serving dish, cover loosely with foil and keep hot.

Skim the fat from the juices in the roasting tin, then bring to the boil on top of the stove. Stir in the rest of the mustard, lemon juice, sugar and the orange juice. Taste and adjust the seasoning.

Garnish the lamb with watercress and serve with Brussels sprouts or peas, plain potatoes boiled in their skins, and the gravy. This meat is also good cold with a salad.

Variation:
Breast of lamb may be substituted for shoulder. It is much cheaper but fatty, so be prepared to trim it well.

Lamb and pea stew with dumplings

Preparation time: 25 minutes
Cooking time: 2½–3 hours
Oven 160°C, 325°F, Gas Mark 3

25 g butter
1 × 15 ml spoon olive oil
1 onion, peeled and chopped
500 g lean lamb e.g. leg fillet, trimmed of excess fat and cubed
1 leek, trimmed and chopped
1 parsnip, peeled and chopped
1 turnip, peeled and chopped
4 carrots, scraped and chopped
450 g peas
about 900 ml hot water
2 × 5 ml spoons pot barley
3–4 fresh mint leaves, chopped, or 1 × 5 ml spoon dried mint
1 × 2.5 ml spoon dried rosemary, or 1 fresh rosemary sprig
sea salt
freshly ground black pepper
chopped fresh parsley, to garnish

1 oz butter
1 tablespoon olive oil
1 onion, peeled and chopped
1¼ lb lean lamb e.g. leg fillet, trimmed of excess fat and cubed
1 leek, trimmed and chopped
1 parsnip, peeled and chopped
1 turnip, peeled and chopped
4 carrots, scraped and chopped
1 lb peas
about 1½ pints hot water
2 teaspoons pot barley
3–4 fresh mint leaves, chopped, or 1 teaspoon dried mint
½ teaspoon dried rosemary, or 1 fresh rosemary sprig
sea salt
freshly ground black pepper
chopped fresh parsley, to garnish

Dumplings:
75 g self-raising wholemeal flour
1 × 2.5 ml spoon fine sea salt
1 small onion, peeled and grated or very finely chopped
40 g vegetable fat, cut into small pieces
2–3 × 15 ml spoons cold water

Dumplings:
3 oz self-raising wholemeal flour
½ teaspoon fine sea salt
1 small onion, peeled and grated or very finely chopped
1½ oz vegetable fat, cut into small pieces
2–3 tablespoons cold water

Pot barley is available from most health food shops. It is the whole barley and much better than pearl barley, which is refined. This casserole is particularly delicious if it is made in advance and re-heated.

Melt the butter with the oil in a large flameproof casserole, add the onion and fry gently until it is lightly browned. Remove the onion. Add the lamb and brown on all sides. Return the onion to the casserole with the leek, parsnip, turnip, carrots and 350 g/12 oz of the peas, if using fresh. Stir the vegetables in the hot fat for 1–2 minutes, then pour over just enough hot water to cover completely.
Bring to the boil, skimming if necessary, then add the pot barley, mint, rosemary, and salt and pepper. Cover tightly and transfer to a preheated oven. Cook for 2½–3 hours or until the meat is tender. Check the stew after about 1½ hours to ensure that there is still enough liquid to cover the contents, adding a little more hot water if necessary.
About 30 minutes before the stew is ready, make the dumplings. Sift the flour and salt into a mixing bowl, tipping in any bran left in the sieve. Stir in the onion, then mix in the fat with a knife. Add just enough water to bind the mixture. Roll into dumplings the size of a large walnut.
Add the dumplings to the stew with the rest of the fresh peas, or all of the peas if using frozen, for the last 15 minutes' cooking time. Cover tightly. Taste and adjust the seasoning, then sprinkle with parsley.
Serves 6

Variation:
This can be made with 4–5 potatoes, peeled and diced, instead of dumplings. Add the potatoes with the other vegetables.

Lamb kebabs

Preparation time: 15 minutes, plus marinating
Cooking time: 12–15 minutes

Metric

1 × 1¼ kg leg or shoulder of lamb, boned and cubed
1 green pepper, cored, seeded and diced
1 small onion, peeled and quartered
3 tomatoes, quartered

Marinade:

2 × 5 ml spoons sunflower or olive oil
3 × 15 ml spoons Natural Yogurt (page 8)
juice of 2 lemons
2 garlic cloves, peeled and crushed
1 × 5 ml spoon dried mint or 3–4 fresh mint leaves, chopped
1 × 2.5 ml spoon dried rosemary or 1 fresh rosemary sprig
1 × 1.25 ml spoon sea salt
freshly ground black pepper
1 × 5 ml spoon paprika
1 × 1.25 ml spoon dry mustard

Imperial

1 × 2½ lb leg or shoulder of lamb, boned and cubed
1 green pepper, cored, seeded and diced
1 small onion, peeled and quartered
3 tomatoes, quartered

Marinade:

2 teaspoons sunflower or olive oil
3 tablespoons Natural Yogurt (page 8)
juice of 2 lemons
2 garlic cloves, peeled and crushed
1 teaspoon dried mint or 3–4 fresh mint leaves, chopped
½ teaspoon dried rosemary or 1 fresh rosemary sprig
¼ teaspoon sea salt
freshly ground black pepper
1 teaspoon paprika
¼ teaspoon dry mustard

This is a very quick dish to assemble once the meat has been marinated. Leg of lamb is dear, but there is little waste. The butcher will usually bone the leg or shoulder and if you ask for the bone it can be used for soup – see Lamb Broth (page 20).

Combine all the marinade ingredients in a shallow bowl. Stir well, then add the cubed lamb. Cover and leave to marinate for at least 6 hours, or preferably overnight.

When ready to cook, drain the lamb cubes, reserving any marinade. Thread the lamb cubes on to greased skewers with the green pepper, onion and tomatoes. Cook under a preheated grill for about 12 minutes, turning and brushing with the reserved marinade. Serve with Boiled Brown Rice (page 34).

Lamb and pea stew with dumplings;
Lamb kebabs

Liver with tomatoes and green peppers

Metric	Imperial
3 × 15 ml spoons olive oil or 40 g butter	3 tablespoons olive oil or 1½ oz butter
1 large onion, peeled and chopped	1 large onion, peeled and chopped
2 green peppers, cored, seeded and chopped	2 green peppers, cored, seeded and chopped
2 garlic cloves, peeled and finely chopped	2 garlic cloves, peeled and finely chopped
450 g tomatoes, peeled and chopped, or 1 × 400 g can tomatoes, drained	1 lb tomatoes, peeled and chopped, or 1 × 14 oz can tomatoes, drained
1 × 2.5 ml spoon dried oregano	½ teaspoon dried oregano
1 × 2.5 ml spoon dried basil	½ teaspoon dried basil
2 × 5 ml spoons tomato purée	2 teaspoons tomato purée
2 drops Tabasco sauce	2 drops Tabasco sauce
sea salt	sea salt
freshly ground black pepper	freshly ground black pepper
450 g lamb's liver, thinly sliced	1 lb lamb's liver, thinly sliced

Preparation time: 15 minutes
Cooking time: 20–25 minutes

Heat 2 × 15 ml spoons/2 tablespoons of the oil or melt 25 g/1 oz of the butter, in a large frying pan. Add the onion and fry until translucent. Add the green peppers and garlic and continue to fry gently until the peppers are soft. Add the tomatoes and fry for 2 minutes, then stir in the herbs, tomato purée, Tabasco sauce and salt and pepper. Continue cooking for about 5 minutes.

Meanwhile, heat the remaining oil or butter in another frying pan. Add the sliced liver and fry for 2–3 minutes or until lightly browned on both sides, and cooked through.

Add the liver to the vegetable mixture and stir in gently. Taste and adjust the seasoning, then serve immediately.

Kidney stroganoff

Metric	Imperial
15 g butter	½ oz butter
1 × 15 ml spoon olive oil	1 tablespoon olive oil
1 onion, peeled and chopped	1 onion, peeled and chopped
450 g lamb's kidneys, skinned, cored and thinly sliced	1 lb lamb's kidneys, skinned, cored and thinly sliced
225 g mushrooms, chopped	8 oz mushrooms, chopped
sea salt	sea salt
freshly ground black pepper	freshly ground black pepper
150 ml soured cream	¼ pint soured cream
1 × 15 ml spoon brandy	1 tablespoon brandy
pinch of ground cinnamon	pinch of ground cinnamon
pinch of grated nutmeg	pinch of grated nutmeg

Preparation time: 15 minutes
Cooking time: 25 minutes

This is a cheaper version of the more extravagant dish that uses fillet of beef. If soured cream is not available, use half double cream and half Natural Yogurt (page 8). If you can find tiny button mushrooms, use them whole.

Melt the butter with the oil in a large frying pan, add the onion and fry until golden. Remove the onion from the pan and keep hot. Add the kidneys to the pan and fry gently until lightly browned. Add the mushrooms and cook for a further 2–3 minutes, stirring. Return the onions to the pan with salt and pepper. Stir, then cover tightly and simmer very gently for about 10 minutes or until there is no more red juice left from the kidneys.

Stir in the soured cream, brandy, cinnamon and nutmeg. Heat through gently, but do not allow to boil or the sauce may curdle. Taste and adjust the seasoning, then serve, with potatoes, boiled in their skins and sliced, or with Boiled Brown Rice (page 34) and a green salad.

Kidney stroganoff; Stir-fried liver with Chinese leaves; Liver with tomatoes and green peppers

Stir-fried liver with Chinese leaves

Preparation time: 10 minutes
Cooking time: 10 minutes

Melt 15 g/½ oz of the butter in a frying pan, add the ginger and garlic and fry gently for about 2 minutes. Sprinkle on the sesame seeds and cook for a further minute, stirring. Add the cabbage and spring onions, and continue to fry gently, stirring frequently, for about 5 minutes.

Meanwhile, melt the rest of the butter in another frying pan, add the liver and fry for 2 minutes. Add the sherry and fry for a further minute until the liver is lightly browned and cooked through.

Add the liver to the cabbage mixture with salt and pepper to taste. Mix together gently. Serve with ribbon noodles or wholemeal macaroni.

Metric
40 g butter
5 cm fresh ginger root, peeled and chopped
1 garlic clove, peeled and finely chopped
1 × 15 ml spoon sesame seeds
1 firm medium Chinese cabbage trimmed of stalk and the leaves finely chopped
about 150 g spring onions, chopped
450 g lamb's liver, very thinly sliced
2 × 15 ml spoons dry sherry
sea salt
freshly ground black pepper

Imperial
1½ oz butter
2 inch fresh ginger root, peeled and chopped
1 garlic clove, peeled and finely chopped
1 tablespoon sesame seeds
1 firm medium Chinese cabbage trimmed of stalk and the leaves finely chopped
about 5 oz spring onions chopped
1 lb lamb's liver, very thinly sliced
2 tablespoons dry sherry
sea salt
freshly ground black pepper

Chicken in a brick with lemon and marjoram

Metric	*Imperial*
1 × 1½ kg roasting chicken	1 × 3½ lb roasting chicken
thinly pared rind and juice of ½ lemon	thinly pared rind and juice of ½ lemon
1 × 5 ml spoon sea salt	1 teaspoon sea salt
2 × 5 ml spoons dried marjoram	2 teaspoons dried marjoram
1 garlic clove, peeled and finely chopped (optional)	1 garlic clove, peeled and finely chopped (optional)
freshly ground black pepper	freshly ground black pepper

Preparation time: 5–10 minutes, plus soaking time
Cooking time: 1½ hours
Oven: 220°C, 425°F, Gas Mark 7

Chicken bricks are inexpensive to buy and easy to use. Follow the directions for your own brick – usually it must be soaked in cold water for 10 minutes before use and put into a cold oven, rather than a preheated one. If you prefer just a suggestion of garlic, rub the inside of the brick with the garlic clove, rather than chopping and inserting it into the chicken skin. Chicken cooked in a brick is succulent without any addition of fat or liquid.

Soak the brick in cold water for 10 minutes, or according to the directions. Meanwhile, prepare the chicken. Put the strip of lemon rind, the salt and 1 × 5 ml spoon/1 teaspoon of the marjoram inside the chicken. Make small incisions in the chicken skin with a knife and insert the chopped garlic, if using. Rub the rest of the marjoram, and pepper, over the chicken. Drain the water from the brick, put in the chicken, cover with the lid and place in a cold oven. Switch on the oven and cook for 1½ hours. Remove the lid for the last 20–30 minutes if you like, to brown the outside. Remove the chicken from the brick and place it on a warmed serving platter. Skim the fat from the juices left in the brick and pour the juices into a small pan. Add the lemon juice and bring to the boil. Taste and adjust the seasoning, then pour into a gravy boat and hand round with the carved chicken. Ratatouille (page 64) makes a delicious accompaniment.

Chicken dhansak

Preparation time: 1 hour
Cooking time: about 2 hours

Metric	*Imperial*
350 g split red lentils, rinsed and drained	*12 oz split red lentils, rinsed and drained*
1.5 litres cold water	*2½ pints cold water*
1 bay leaf	*1 bay leaf*
1 × 5 ml spoon sea salt	*1 teaspoon sea salt*
6 × 15 ml spoons olive oil or 75 g butter	*6 tablespoons olive oil or 3 oz butter*
2 large onions, peeled and chopped	*2 large onions, peeled and chopped*
5 cm fresh ginger root, peeled and finely chopped, or 2 × 5 ml spoons ground ginger	*2 inch fresh ginger root, peeled and finely chopped, or 2 teaspoons ground ginger*
4 garlic cloves, peeled and chopped	*4 garlic cloves, peeled and chopped*
8 chicken pieces, skinned	*8 chicken pieces, skinned*
1 large aubergine, diced	*1 large aubergine, diced*
450 g tomatoes, peeled and chopped, or 1 × 400 g can tomatoes	*1 lb tomatoes, peeled and chopped, or 1 × 14 oz can tomatoes*
1 × 5 ml spoon tomato purée	*1 teaspoon tomato purée*
1 × 15 ml spoon chopped fresh mint leaves	*1 tablespoon chopped fresh mint leaves*
1 × 5 ml spoon chilli powder	*1 teaspoon chilli powder*
1 × 1.25 ml spoon ground cloves	*¼ teaspoon ground cloves*
1 × 5 ml spoon ground cinnamon or 1 × 5 cm cinnamon stick	*1 teaspoon ground cinnamon or 1 × 2 inch cinnamon stick*
1 × 2.5 ml spoon ground cardamom or 4 whole green cardamoms	*½ teaspoon ground cardamom or 4 whole green cardamoms*
1 × 5 ml spoon turmeric	*1 teaspoon turmeric*
1 × 5 ml spoon ground coriander	*1 teaspoon ground coriander*
1 × 5 ml spoon ground cumin	*1 teaspoon ground cumin*
few chopped fresh coriander leaves, to garnish	*few chopped fresh coriander leaves, to garnish*

This is a classic Parsee dish. Traditionally, it is quite hot, but you can use less chilli powder, according to taste. Different brands of chilli powder vary in strength. A blender is needed to make the sauce.

Put the lentils into a deep saucepan or flameproof casserole and pour over the cold water. Bring to the boil, skimming if necessary, then add the bay leaf and salt. Cover tightly and simmer for 30–40 minutes or until the lentils are soft. The lentils will absorb most of the water while cooking.

Heat half of the olive oil, or half of the butter in a large frying pan. Add one chopped onion and fry gently until transparent. Add half the ginger and two cloves of garlic and fry gently until the onion and garlic are browned, stirring constantly. Put in the chicken pieces and continue to fry until they are well browned on all sides.

Transfer the contents of the frying pan to the cooked lentils and their liquor. Add the aubergine, tomatoes and tomato purée. There should be enough liquid to cover the chicken; if not, add a little more water. Stir the mixture and bring to the boil. Cover tightly and simmer gently for about 40 minutes or until the chicken is tender. Stir frequently to prevent the lentils from sticking to the bottom of the pan.

Remove the chicken pieces from the pan and set on one side. Discard the bay leaf. Add the mint to the lentil mixture, put into a blender goblet and blend to a smooth, thick purée. Set on one side.

Heat the rest of the oil or butter in a pan, add the remaining chopped onion and fry until browned. Add the rest of the ginger and garlic and fry gently for 2 minutes, then stir in the chilli powder and fry for a further 1 minute. Add the cloves, cinnamon, cardamom, turmeric, ground coriander and cumin and fry gently for 5–10 minutes, stirring frequently. Add a little more oil or butter if necessary.

Stir the lentil purée into the spicy onion mixture. Bring to the boil. The sauce should be fairly thick, so if it seems too liquid, simmer uncovered for a few minutes. Cover tightly and simmer for 10 minutes.

Cut the chicken into small pieces, discarding the bones. Add to the lentil sauce and simmer for a further 10–15 minutes, stirring frequently. Taste and adjust the seasoning.

Sprinkle with fresh coriander and serve hot, with Brown Rice with Almonds (page 34) and a salad. Another good accompaniment is a side dish of 1 large banana, sliced and mixed with 150 ml/¼ pint Natural Yogurt (page 8) and a little ground cardamom.
Serves 6–8

Chicken dhansak;
Chicken in a brick with lemon and marjoram

Chicken with leeks

Metric	Imperial
6 chicken pieces	6 chicken pieces
1 carrot, scraped	1 carrot, scraped
1 onion, peeled	1 onion, peeled
1 celery stick	1 celery stick
1 bay leaf	1 bay leaf
1 parsley sprig	1 parsley sprig
sea salt	sea salt
5 black peppercorns	5 black peppercorns
25 g butter	1 oz butter
750 g leeks, trimmed and chopped	1½ lb leeks, trimmed and chopped
1 × 15 ml spoon plain wholemeal flour	1 tablespoon plain wholemeal flour
1 × 450 g jar pickled dill cucumbers, drained and sliced, reserving 2 × 15 ml spoons liquor	1 × 1 lb jar pickled dill cucumbers, drained and sliced, reserving 2 tablespoons liquor
juice of ½ lemon	juice of ½ lemon
1 × 5 ml spoon dried dill	1 teaspoon dried dill
pinch of demerara sugar, or more to taste	pinch of demerara sugar, or more to taste
150 ml soured cream	¼ pint soured cream
freshly ground black pepper	freshly ground black pepper

Preparation time: 20 minutes
Cooking time: about 1½ hours

The chicken is served in a delicate, sweet-sour sauce and any cooking liquid left over after making the sauce will make an excellent base for a soup. Pickled dill cucumbers are available from some greengrocers and many supermarkets.

Put the chicken pieces into a large saucepan with the carrot, onion and celery. Pour in enough water to cover completely. Bring to the boil and skim. Add the bay leaf, parsley, salt and peppercorns. Cover and simmer gently for about 1¼ hours or until tender. Remove the chicken pieces from the pan and skin them. Keep them hot. Strain the cooking liquid into a jug. Melt the butter in a large saucepan or flame-proof casserole, add the leeks, cover tightly and fry gently for about 8 minutes. Shake the pan occasionally to prevent the leeks sticking. Remove the lid and sprinkle over the flour. Cook, stirring, for a further 1 minute, then stir in 150 ml/¼ pint of the reserved cooking liquid. Simmer until thickened. Put in the chicken pieces and reheat thoroughly. Add a little more of the cooking liquid, if necessary, but keep the sauce thick.
Add the pickled cucumbers with the reserved liquor from the jar, the lemon juice, dill and sugar. Stir in the soured cream and heat through gently without boiling. Taste and adjust the seasoning and serve.

Chicken with chick peas

Metric	Imperial
225 g dried chick peas, soaked overnight	8 oz dried chick peas, soaked overnight
3 × 15 ml spoons olive oil	3 tablespoons olive oil
4 chicken portions (about 1 kg)	4 chicken portions (about 2 lb)
2 large onions, peeled and chopped	2 large onions, peeled and chopped
2 garlic cloves, peeled and finely chopped	2 garlic cloves, peeled and finely chopped
2 celery sticks, chopped	2 celery sticks, chopped
1½–2 × 15 ml spoons paprika	1½–2 tablespoons paprika
1 × 2.5 ml spoon cayenne	½ teaspoon cayenne
sea salt	sea salt
freshly ground black pepper	freshly ground black pepper
200 ml hot Stock (page 16) or water	⅓ pint hot Stock (page 16) or water
2 × 5 ml spoons tomato purée	2 teaspoons tomato purée
juice of 1 lemon	juice of 1 lemon
1 green pepper, cored, seeded and thinly sliced	1 green pepper, cored, seeded and thinly sliced
1 red pepper, cored, seeded and thinly sliced, or 1 canned pimento, sliced	1 red pepper, cored, seeded and thinly sliced, or 1 canned red pimento, sliced
chopped fresh parsley, to garnish	chopped fresh parsley, to garnish

Preparation time: 25 minutes, plus overnight soaking
Cooking time: 2½–3½ hours
Oven: 160°C, 325°F, Gas Mark 3

Drain the chick peas and put them into a saucepan. Cover with fresh cold water, bring to the boil and boil for 10 minutes. Cover and simmer for 1–2 hours or until tender. Drain.
Heat the oil in a large flameproof casserole, add the chicken portions and fry until well browned on all sides. Remove from the casserole and set aside. Add the onions to the casserole and fry until brown, stirring occasionally. Add the garlic and celery and continue to fry gently for 2 minutes. Add the chick peas and fry for a further 2–3 minutes.
Stir in the paprika, cayenne, and salt and pepper to taste, then pour over the hot stock or water and stir in the tomato purée and lemon juice. Add the sliced pepper and bring to the boil.
Return the chicken to the casserole, cover tightly and transfer to a preheated oven. Cook for 1¼ hours or until the chicken is tender.
Sprinkle with parsley and serve with Boiled Brown Rice (page 34) and a green salad.

Chicken with leeks; Chicken with chick peas; Stuffed chicken

Stuffed chicken

Metric
1 × 1½ kg roasting
  chicken
150 ml water
1 × 2.5 ml spoon paprika

Marinade:
50 g sultanas
50 g blanched almonds
1 × 15 ml spoon honey
juice of 1 lemon
1 × 5 ml spoon dried
  tarragon
1 × 2.5 ml spoon paprika
1 × 2.5 ml spoon sea salt
1 × 1.25 ml spoon dry
  mustard
300 ml Natural Yogurt
  (page 8)
1 garlic clove, crushed

Stuffing:
1 × 15 ml spoon olive oil
1 onion, peeled and
  chopped
50 g burghul wheat,
  soaked in water for
  30 minutes, drained
sea salt
freshly ground black
  pepper
1 × 5 ml spoon dried
  tarragon

Imperial
1 × 3½ lb roasting
  chicken
¼ pint water
½ teaspoon paprika

Marinade:
2 oz sultanas
2 oz blanched almonds
1 tablespoon honey
juice of 1 lemon
1 teaspoon dried
  tarragon
½ teaspoon paprika
½ teaspoon sea salt
¼ teaspoon dry
  mustard
½ pint Natural Yogurt
  page 8)
1 garlic clove, crushed

Stuffing:
1 tablespoon olive oil
1 onion, peeled and
  chopped
2 oz burghul wheat,
  soaked in water for
  30 minutes, drained
sea salt
freshly ground black
  pepper
1 teaspoon dried
  tarragon

Preparation time: 10–15 minutes, plus soaking and overnight marinating
Cooking time: about 1½ hours
Oven: 190°C, 375°F, Gas Mark 5

The chicken is marinated, then stuffed and cooked in a rich-tasting yet low-fat sauce. This recipe does require a blender for the marinade. Burghul wheat is also known as bulgur and tabbouleh: it is toasted, cracked wheat and can be found in health food shops and Greek food stores.

To make the marinade, put the sultanas, almonds, honey, lemon juice, tarragon, paprika, salt, mustard and 150 ml/¼ pint of the yogurt into a blender goblet and blend for a few seconds until smooth. Stir in the rest of the yogurt and the garlic.
Put the chicken in a bowl, pour over the marinade, cover and leave to marinate overnight in the refrigerator, turning the chicken over from time to time whenever possible.
The next day, remove the chicken from the refrigerator 30 minutes before cooking. Meanwhile, prepare the stuffing. Heat the oil in a small frying pan, add the onion and fry until transparent. Add the burghul wheat and fry until lightly browned, stirring constantly. Add salt and pepper, then stir in the tarragon and 2 × 15 ml spoons/2 tablespoons of the marinade. Stuff this mixture into the chicken and place it in a roasting tin. Spoon over any marinade left in the original bowl and pour the water over. Dust with the paprika, then cover with buttered paper and cook in a preheated oven for about 1½ hours or until the chicken is cooked through.
Serve with Brown Rice with Almonds (page 34) and a salad.

51

Haddock with prawns in tomato sauce

Metric
4 haddock fillets (about 750 g)
sea salt
freshly ground black pepper
juice of 1 lemon
1 parsley sprig
1 bay leaf
chopped fresh parsley, to garnish

Sauce:
2 × 15 ml spoons olive oil
1 onion, peeled and chopped
2 garlic cloves, peeled and finely chopped
450 g tomatoes, peeled and chopped
1 × 5 ml spoon tomato purée
1 parsley sprig
1 bay leaf
1 × 5 ml spoon dried oregano
sea salt
freshly ground black pepper
100 g peeled prawns

Imperial
4 haddock fillets (about 1½ lb)
sea salt
freshly ground black pepper
juice of 1 lemon
1 parsley sprig
1 bay leaf
chopped fresh parsley, to garnish

Sauce:
2 tablespoons olive oil
1 onion, peeled and chopped
2 garlic cloves, peeled and finely chopped
1 lb tomatoes, peeled and chopped
1 teaspoon tomato purée
1 parsley sprig
1 bay leaf
1 teaspoon dried oregano
sea salt
freshly ground black pepper
4 oz peeled prawns

Preparation time: 10–15 minutes
Cooking time: 20 minutes
Oven: 180°C, 350°F, Gas Mark 4

First prepare the sauce. Heat the olive oil in a saucepan, add the onion and garlic, and fry until transparent. Add the remaining sauce ingredients except the prawns, and stir well. Cover tightly and simmer over a low heat for 15 minutes.

Meanwhile, put the fish into a buttered ovenproof dish, add salt and pepper and pour over the lemon juice. Add the parsley sprig and bay leaf, cover with well-buttered paper and cook in a preheated oven for about 15 minutes or until the fish flakes easily when tested with a fork. Add the prawns to the sauce and simmer for 5 minutes.

Arrange the fish on a warmed serving dish. Discard the bay leaf from the sauce. Taste and adjust the seasoning, then spoon over the fish and sprinkle with parsley.

Haddock with prawns in tomato sauce;
Herrings in oatmeal; Mackerel with gooseberry sauce

Herrings in oatmeal

Metric
4 herrings, heads removed, gutted and filleted
juice of ½ lemon
sea salt
freshly ground black pepper
4 × 15 ml spoons medium oatmeal or porridge oats
50 g vegetable fat or 4 × 15 ml spoons olive or nut oil
2 × 15 ml spoons chopped fresh parsley
lemon wedges, to serve

Imperial
4 herrings, heads removed, gutted and filleted
juice of ½ lemon
sea salt
freshly ground black pepper
4 tablespoons medium oatmeal or porridge oats
2 oz vegetable fat or 4 tablespoons olive or nut oil
2 tablespoons chopped fresh parsley
lemon wedges, to serve

Preparation time: 10–15 minutes
Cooking time: about 10 minutes

Make sure that all fine bones have been removed from the herrings, then wipe the fish with paper towel and sprinkle with the lemon juice, salt and pepper. Put the oats on a plate and roll each fillet in them, patting down the oats so that the fish are evenly coated on both sides.

Melt the fat or heat the oil in a frying pan, add the herrings and fry for 3–5 minutes or until golden brown. Turn the fish over and brown the other side. Drain the fish on paper towel, then arrange on a warmed serving dish. Sprinkle with the parsley and garnish with wedges of lemon. Wholemeal bread goes well with this, or new potatoes, boiled in their skins and tossed with butter and chopped fresh parsley.

Mackerel with gooseberry sauce

Metric
4 mackerel, gutted
sea salt
freshly ground black
　pepper
juice of 1 lemon
lemon wedges, to garnish

Sauce:
225 g gooseberries, topped
　and tailed
3 × 15 ml spoons boiling
　water
sea salt
freshly ground black
　pepper
pinch of ground ginger
1 × 15 ml spoon Barbados
　sugar

Imperial
4 mackerel, gutted
sea salt
freshly ground black
　pepper
juice of 1 lemon
lemon wedges, to garnish

Sauce:
8 oz gooseberries, topped
　and tailed
3 tablespoons boiling
　water
sea salt
freshly ground black
　pepper
pinch of ground ginger
1 tablespoon Barbados
　sugar

Preparation time: 15 minutes
Cooking time: about 15 minutes

Combine all the ingredients for the sauce in a small saucepan and heat gently, stirring constantly, until the fruit is a pulp. Allow to cool slightly, then sieve the mixture, using a nylon sieve. Return to the pan and reheat gently. Taste and adjust the seasoning, also adding more sugar if necessary. Keep warm.
Make 3–4 diagonal cuts across the backbone of each side of the mackerel, then sprinkle salt, pepper and lemon juice on the inside and outside. Cook under a preheated grill for 5–8 minutes on each side or until the fish is well browned and will flake easily when tested with a fork.
Garnish the fish with lemon wedges. Serve with the gooseberry sauce, and new potatoes, boiled in their skins. Cauliflower with Garlic and Almonds (page 69) makes a good accompaniment.

Plaice florentine

Metric	Imperial
1 kg fresh spinach, large stalks removed, chopped	2 lb fresh spinach, large stalks removed, chopped
sea salt	sea salt
freshly ground black pepper	freshly ground black pepper
8 plaice fillets	8 plaice fillets
25 g Parmesan cheese, grated	1 oz Parmesan cheese, grated
15 g butter	½ oz butter
1 × 5 ml spoon paprika	1 teaspoon paprika

Cheese sauce:	Cheese sauce:
25 g butter	1 oz butter
2 × 15 ml spoons plain wholemeal flour	2 tablespoons plain wholemeal flour
300 ml hot milk	½ pint hot milk
25 g Cheddar cheese, grated	1 oz Cheddar cheese, grated
sea salt	sea salt
freshly ground black pepper	freshly ground black pepper
pinch of grated nutmeg	pinch of grated nutmeg
1 egg yolk	1 egg yolk
1 × 5 ml spoon cold milk	1 teaspoon cold milk

Preparation time: 25–35 minutes
Cooking time: 40–45 minutes
Oven: 190°C, 375°F, Gas Mark 5

Put the spinach into a pan, add a little salt and pepper, and cover with a tightly fitting lid. Do not add any water: there should be enough still clinging to the leaves from their washing. Cook over a gentle heat for 10 minutes. Shake the pan occasionally to make sure that the spinach does not stick to the bottom.

Drain the spinach, pressing out all excess moisture, and spread it over the bottom of a buttered baking dish. Lay the fish fillets on top.

To make the sauce, melt the 25g/1 oz butter in a saucepan and stir in the flour. Cook, stirring, for 1–2 minutes, then gradually stir in the hot milk. Simmer, stirring, until the sauce is thick and smooth. Add the Cheddar cheese and stir until it has melted. Add salt, pepper and the nutmeg, and remove from the heat.

Put the egg yolk into a cup with 1 × 15 ml spoon/1 tablespoon of the hot cheese sauce and the cold milk. Stir until well mixed, then add to the remaining hot sauce. Stir well, then pour over the fish.

Sprinkle over the Parmesan cheese, dot with the butter and dust with the paprika. Cook in a preheated oven for 20–25 minutes or until the top is browned and bubbling. Serve with a tomato salad.

Sole with fennel and soured cream sauce

Metric	Imperial
150 ml dry white wine or cider	¼ pint dry white wine or cider
sea salt	sea salt
freshly ground black pepper	freshly ground black pepper
2 × 5 ml spoons Barbados sugar	2 teaspoons Barbados sugar
2 heads of fennel, trimmed and diced	2 heads of fennel, trimmed and diced
4 Dover or lemon sole, filleted	4 Dover or lemon sole, filleted
juice of 1 lemon	juice of 1 lemon

Sauce:	Sauce:
15 g butter	½ oz butter
1 × 15 ml spoon plain wholemeal flour	1 tablespoon plain wholemeal flour
1–2 × 15 ml spoons chopped fresh fennel leaves	1–2 tablespoons chopped fresh fennel leaves
150 ml soured cream	¼ pint soured cream
pinch of ground cinnamon	pinch of ground cinnamon
sea salt	sea salt
freshly ground black pepper	freshly ground black pepper

Preparation time: 15 minutes
Cooking time: about 30 minutes
Oven: 180°C, 350°F, Gas Mark 4

Put the wine or cider in a saucepan and bring to the boil. Add salt, pepper and the sugar, then stir in the diced fennel. Cover tightly and simmer for 5 minutes. Meanwhile, put the fish fillets in a buttered ovenproof serving dish. Pour over the fennel and its cooking juice and add the lemon juice. Cover with foil and cook in a preheated oven for about 20 minutes or until the fish flakes easily when tested with a fork.

Strain the juices into a jug and keep the fish and fennel hot while you prepare the sauce.

Melt the butter in a small saucepan, stir in the flour and cook, stirring, for 2 minutes. Gradually stir in the cooking juices and bring to the boil. Simmer, stirring, until thick and smooth. Add the chopped fennel leaves and simmer for a further 2–3 minutes. Stir in the soured cream and cinnamon. Taste the sauce and adjust the seasoning, adding more sugar if necessary. Reheat gently, but do not allow to boil. Pour the sauce over the fish and serve.

Cod fillets in cider; Sole with fennel and soured cream ; Plaice florentine

Cod fillets in cider

Metric
4 cod fillets (750 g–1 kg)
½ lemon
2 × 15 ml spoons chopped
  fresh parsley
2 large onions, peeled and
  thinly sliced
2 bay leaves
chopped fresh parsley, to
  garnish

Imperial
4 cod fillets (1½–2 lb)
½ lemon
2 tablespoons chopped
  fresh parsley
2 large onions, peeled and
  thinly sliced
2 bay leaves
chopped fresh parsley, to
  garnish

Marinade:
about 300 ml cider
1 × 2.5 ml spoon
  Barbados sugar
1 × 2.5 ml spoon dry
  mustard
2 drops Worcestershire
  sauce
1 × 2.5 ml spoon ground
  allspice
sea salt
freshly ground black
  pepper
pinch of grated nutmeg

Marinade:
about ½ pint cider
½ teaspoon Barbados
  sugar
½ teaspoon dry
  mustard
2 drops Worcestershire
  sauce
½ teaspoon ground
  allspice
sea salt
freshly ground black
  pepper
pinch of grated nutmeg

Preparation time: 10 minutes, plus 2 hours for marinating
Cooking time: 45 minutes – 1 hour
Oven: 160°C, 325°F, Gas Mark 3

Put the cod fillets into an ovenproof dish and rub them with the lemon. Add the parsley, onions and bay leaves to the fish. Mix together all the ingredients for the marinade and pour over the fish. If the liquid does not cover the fish add a little more cider. Cover and leave to marinate at room temperature for about 2 hours.
Put the dish into a preheated oven and cook for 45 minutes – 1 hour. Sprinkle with parsley and serve with new potatoes boiled in their skins, boiled parsnips and Lemon Glazed Carrots (page 66).

SALADS AND VEGETABLES

Fresh vegetables and salads are excellent sources of dietary fibre, vitamins and minerals. Try to select the best quality produce and use it as soon as possible. Vegetables should be cooked in a pan with a tightly fitting lid, for only the minimum of time and in the minimum amount of liquid, which can be retained for making nutritious soups and stock. Serve hot vegetable dishes as quickly as possible after preparation, before both vitamin content and flavour suffer.

Lemon juice contains vitamin C, so it is preferable to vinegar for everyday use in salad dressings. Shred or cut salad ingredients just before use to prevent loss of vitamins.

Salad dressings keep successfully in screw-topped jars in the refrigerator. Try to use an unsaturated sunflower, safflower or corn oil in a dressing (page 58). Unsaturated oils are the type that never thicken or harden, even when refrigerated. Good quality olive oil has an excellent flavour but it is not as rich in beneficial polyunsaturates. Sesame seeds can be fried in a little oil until they start jumping in the pan and turning brown. Sprinkle them over almost any type of salad, especially green salads. Each salad will serve four people as an accompaniment and six people as a starter. To serve these salads as the main dish you may wish to increase the proportions.

Leeks vinaigrette; Spicy cauliflower salad;
Spinach and cheese salad

Spicy cauliflower salad

Metric	Imperial
1 cauliflower, cut into small florets	1 cauliflower, cut into small florets
100 g button mushrooms, thinly sliced	4 oz button mushrooms, thinly sliced
150 ml Mayonnaise (page 58)	¼ pint Mayonnaise (page 58)
1 × 5 ml spoon brown sugar	1 teaspoon brown sugar
2 × 5 ml spoons ground cumin	2 teaspoons ground cumin
1 × 2.5 ml spoon ground cardamom	½ teaspoon ground cardamom
1 × 5 ml spoon ground turmeric	1 teaspoon ground turmeric
1 garlic clove, peeled and crushed	1 garlic clove, peeled and crushed

Preparation time: 10 minutes

This salad is tasty on its own or as a starter. It also makes a good accompaniment to curried dishes, or Tandoori-style Spicy Kebabs (page 40).

Mix the cauliflower and mushrooms together in a salad bowl. Combine all the other ingredients in a small mixing bowl. When thoroughly mixed, pour over the vegetables.

Leeks vinaigrette

Metric	Imperial
4 large or 8 small leeks	4 large or 8 small leeks
about 7 × 15 ml spoons Lemon French Dressing (page 58)	about 7 tablespoons Lemon French Dressing (page 58)
1 × 5 ml spoon wine or cider vinegar	1 teaspoon wine or cider vinegar
1 × 5 ml spoon Barbados sugar or clear honey	1 teaspoon Barbados sugar or clear honey
2 × 15 ml spoons chopped fresh parsley	2 tablespoons chopped fresh parsley
chopped fresh parsley, to garnish	chopped fresh parsley, to garnish

Preparation time: 5 minutes
Cooking time: about 12 minutes

Trim and clean the leeks but retain as much of the green part as possible. Rinse them thoroughly in cold water, then put them into very little boiling salted water and cook for about 12 minutes or until just tender. Drain. Refresh the leeks under a little cold running water and drain well.
Mix all the other ingredients together thoroughly. Arrange the leeks in a long serving dish and pour the dressing over. Scatter with extra chopped fresh parsley, if liked, and serve at once.

Spinach and cheese salad

Metric	Imperial
450 g spinach, trimmed and shredded	1 lb spinach, trimmed and shredded
4 carrots, peeled and cut into matchsticks	4 carrots, peeled and cut into matchsticks
225 g cottage cheese	8 oz cottage cheese
1 punnet mustard and cress	1 punnet mustard and cress
1 × 2.5 ml spoon dried chervil	½ teaspoon dried chervil
1 × 2.5 ml spoon dried lemon balm	½ teaspoon dried lemon balm
6 × 15 ml spoons Lemon French Dressing (page 58)	about 6 tablespoons Lemon French Dressing (page 58)

Preparation time: 5–10 minutes

Put the spinach in a serving bowl, arrange the carrots around the edge and put the cottage cheese in the centre. Sprinkle with mustard and cress.
Mix the herbs with the dressing and pour over the salad just before serving, or hand the dressing round separately.

Mayonnaise

Metric	Imperial
2 egg yolks	2 egg yolks
juice of ½ lemon	juice of ½ lemon
1 × 2.5 ml spoon dry mustard	½ teaspoon dry mustard
sea salt	sea salt
freshly ground black pepper	freshly ground black pepper
scant 300 ml sunflower oil	scant ½ pint sunflower oil
1 × 15 ml spoon boiling water	1 tablespoon boiling water

Preparation time: 10 minutes

When making mayonnaise all the ingredients should be at room temperature and it is important that the oil is added drop by drop at first. Mayonnaise can also be quickly made in an electric blender. Follow the instructions below but begin with 1 whole egg, instead of the 2 egg yolks. This makes a lighter mayonnaise and also one that is lower in cholesterol. For 'beat' in the hand-beaten recipe, substitute 'blend at top speed'.

Put the egg yolks into a mixing bowl and beat for 2 minutes. Add 2 × 5 ml spoons/2 teaspoons of the lemon juice, the mustard and salt and pepper, and beat again for another 30 seconds. Start adding the oil a drop at a time, beating continuously. When about half the oil has been added, the mayonnaise should start to thicken, and the oil may be added a little faster – about 1 × 15 ml spoon/1 tablespoon at a time. If the mayonnaise becomes too thick, beat in a little more lemon juice with the oil. When all the oil has been incorporated, taste the mayonnaise and adjust the seasoning, adding more lemon juice if necessary. Finally, beat in the boiling water: this will prevent the mayonnaise from curdling, and also help it to keep. If the mayonnaise curdles or will not thicken it can still be saved. Put 1 × 15 ml spoon/1 tablespoon of the curdled mayonnaise into a slightly warmed mixing bowl with 1 × 5 ml spoon/1 teaspoon made mustard. Whisk together until thick, then add the remaining curdled mayonnaise drop by drop, beating well between each addition and making sure that the sauce is thick before adding the next drop. Take care to add the mayonnaise cautiously, especially at first.
Use the mayonnaise immediately, or transfer it to a screw-top jar or airtight container and keep in the refrigerator.
Makes 300 ml/½ pint

Lemon French dressing

Metric	Imperial
3 × 15 ml spoons oil	3 tablespoons oil
1 × 15 ml spoon lemon juice	1 tablespoon lemon juice
pinch of sea salt	pinch of sea salt
freshly ground black pepper	freshly ground black pepper
1 × 15 ml spoon chopped fresh mixed herbs or 1 × 2.5 ml spoon dried mixed herbs	1 tablespoon chopped fresh mixed herbs or ½ teaspoon dried mixed herbs
1 garlic clove, peeled and crushed (optional)	1 garlic clove, peeled and crushed (optional)
1 × 1.25 ml spoon dry mustard	¼ teaspoon dry mustard

Preparation time: 5 minutes

If you wish to make a larger quantity for future use the dressing keeps well in the refrigerator.

Put all the ingredients into a screw-top jar, put the lid on and shake vigorously until the dressing is thoroughly combined.
Makes 50 ml/2 fl oz or 4 × 15 ml spoons/4 tablespoons dressing

Tomato and avocado salad

Metric	Imperial
450 g tomatoes, sliced	1 lb tomatoes, sliced
1 ripe avocado, peeled, stoned and sliced	1 ripe avocado, peeled, stoned and sliced
2 spring onions, finely chopped	2 spring onions, finely chopped
about 7 × 15 ml spoons Lemon French Dressing (above)	about 7 tablespoons Lemon French Dressing (above)
1 × 2.5 ml spoon wine or cider vinegar	½ teaspoon wine or cider vinegar
1 × 2.5 ml spoon Barbados sugar	½ teaspoon Barbados sugar
1 × 2.5 ml spoon dried oregano	½ teaspoon dried oregano
1 garlic clove, peeled and crushed (optional)	1 garlic clove, peeled and crushed (optional)

Preparation time: 10–15 minutes

Put the tomatoes in a serving bowl. Arrange the avocado on top and sprinkle with the spring onions. Mix the dressing with the remaining ingredients and pour over the tomatoes and avocado.

Tomato and avocado salad; Celeriac and apple salad; Lemon French dressing; Mayonnaise

Celeriac and apple salad

Metric
1 head of celeriac (about
   500 g), peeled
juice of 1 lemon
1 eating apple, cored and
   chopped
25 g walnuts, chopped
150 ml double cream
1 × 2.5 ml spoon dry
   mustard
1 × 2.5 ml spoon dried
   lemon thyme
1 × 2.5 ml spoon dried
   thyme
pinch of sea salt
little grated nutmeg
freshly ground black
   pepper
1 × 5 ml spoon Barbados
   sugar
juice of ½ orange

Imperial
1 head of celeriac (about
   1¼ lb), peeled
juice of 1 lemon
1 eating apple, cored and
   chopped
1 oz walnuts, chopped
¼ pint double cream
½ teaspoon dry
   mustard
½ teaspoon dried lemon
   thyme
½ teaspoon dried
   thyme
pinch of sea salt
little grated nutmeg
freshly ground black
   pepper
1 teaspoon Barbados
   sugar
juice of ½ orange

Preparation time: 10–15 minutes

With its creamy-white flesh, celeriac makes an unusual, crunchy salad and tastes similar to celery.

Grate the celeriac into a large bowl and immediately pour over half of the lemon juice. Stir in the apple and walnuts. In a separate small bowl, thoroughly mix the rest of the lemon juice with the remaining ingredients. Pour the cream dressing over the salad, stir well and serve at once.

White bean salad

Metric
225 g dried cannellini or
  haricot beans, soaked
  overnight
1 × 15 ml spoon sunflower
  oil
1 × 5 ml spoon dried
  marjoram or savory
1 garlic clove, peeled and
  crushed
120 ml Lemon French
  Dressing (page
  58)
100 g salami, chopped
  (optional)
1 large or 2 small green
  peppers, cored, seeded
  and chopped
1 onion, peeled and finely
  chopped
sea salt
freshly ground black
  pepper

Imperial
8 oz dried cannellini or
  haricot beans, soaked
  overnight
1 tablespoon sunflower
  oil
1 teaspoon dried
  marjoram or savory
1 garlic clove, peeled and
  crushed
about 4 fl oz Lemon
  French Dressing (page
  58)
4 oz salami, chopped
  (optional)
1 large or 2 small green
  peppers, cored, seeded
  and chopped
1 onion, peeled and finely
  chopped
sea salt
freshly ground black
  pepper

Preparation time: 10 minutes, plus overnight soaking
Cooking time: 1½–2 hours

Put the beans and their soaking liquid in a large heavy
saucepan with the sunflower oil. Do not salt the water
as this toughens the skins. Bring the water slowly to
the boil, cover and boil for 10 minutes, then simmer
gently for 1½–2 hours, or until soft. Add more water
if necessary. Drain the beans.
Mix the herbs and garlic thoroughly with the dressing
and pour over the beans. Allow to cool, then mix with
the salami, if used, green pepper and onion. Taste and
adjust the seasoning before serving.

Egg and asparagus mayonnaise

Metric
450 g fresh asparagus,
  stems peeled, tied in a
  bunch
2–4 eggs, hard-boiled,
  shelled and quartered
150–300 ml Mayonnaise
  (page 58)
chopped fresh parsley, to
  garnish

Imperial
1 lb fresh asparagus,
  stems peeled, tied in a
  bunch
2–4 eggs, hard-boiled,
  shelled and quartered
¼–½ pint Mayonnaise
  (page 58)
chopped fresh parsley, to
  garnish

Preparation time: 10 minutes
Cooking time: 20–25 minutes

This makes a particularly easy and interesting starter
to a special meal.

In a large saucepan, cook the asparagus, uncovered, in
boiling salted water for 10 minutes. Lay the asparagus
down and cook for a further 10–15 minutes, until
tender. Drain and untie.
Put the asparagus in a long, shallow dish. Arrange the
eggs around the asparagus. Pour over the mayonnaise, and sprinkle with parsley.

White bean salad; Egg and asparagus mayonnaise;
Carrot and watercress salad with orange;
Wholewheat salad with coriander

Carrot and watercress salad with orange

Metric	*Imperial*
450 g carrots, scraped and coarsely grated	1 lb carrots, scraped and coarsely grated
2 bunches watercress (about 225 g), chopped	2 bunches watercress (about 8 oz), chopped
1 orange, peeled, sliced and halved	1 orange, peeled sliced and halved

Dressing:	*Dressing:*
4 × 15 ml spoons double cream	4 tablespoons double cream
1 × 15 ml spoon lemon juice	1 tablespoon lemon juice
1 × 1.25 ml spoon dry mustard	¼ teaspoon dry mustard
1 × 1.25 ml spoon sea salt	¼ teaspoon sea salt
freshly ground black pepper	freshly ground black pepper
1 × 2.5 ml spoon clear honey	½ teaspoon clear honey
1 × 5 ml spoon dried marjoram	1 teaspoon dried marjoram
1 × 15 ml spoon sunflower oil	1 tablespoon sunflower oil

Preparation time: 10 minutes

Mix the carrots with the watercress in a large salad bowl. Whisk all the dressing ingredients together and pour over. Arrange the sliced oranges round the outside, adding any juice. Serve at once.

Wholewheat salad with coriander

Metric	*Imperial*
225 g wholewheat grain, soaked overnight	8 oz wholewheat grain, soaked overnight
about 120 ml Lemon French Dressing (page 58)	about 4 fl oz Lemon French Dressing (page 58)
juice of ½ lemon	juice of ½ lemon
2 × 15 ml spoons chopped fresh coriander leaves	2 tablespoons chopped fresh coriander leaves
3 × 15 ml spoons chopped fresh parsley	3 tablespoons chopped fresh parsley
1 garlic clove, peeled and crushed	1 garlic clove, peeled and crushed
1 onion, peeled and chopped	1 onion, peeled and chopped
1 red pepper, cored, seeded and chopped	1 red pepper, cored, seeded and chopped

To garnish:	*To garnish:*
chopped fresh coriander leaves	chopped fresh coriander leaves
chopped fresh parsley	chopped fresh parsley

Preparation time: 5 minutes, plus overnight soaking
Cooking time: 1–1¼ hours

Wholewheat grain can be bought from healthfood shops. It has a nutty flavour which is complemented by the tangy lemon dressing. Asian food stores and some greengrocers sell fresh coriander leaves which have a delicate scent and flavour.

Put the wholewheat and its soaking liquid in a large heavy saucepan, cover and simmer gently for 1–1¼ hours or until soft. Drain and cool completely.
Mix all the remaining ingredients together thoroughly and stir into the wholewheat. Sprinkle with parsley and coriander leaves.

Courgette and potato salad

Metric	Imperial
450 g courgettes, sliced	*1 lb courgettes, sliced*
2 potatoes, peeled or scrubbed	*2 potatoes, peeled or scrubbed*
1 small onion, peeled and finely chopped	*1 small onion, peeled and finely chopped*
2 eggs, hard-boiled and quartered	*2 eggs, hard-boiled and quartered*
150–300 ml Mayonnaise (page 58)	*¼–½ pint Mayonnaise (page 58)*
6 black olives, stoned	*6 black olives, stoned*
1 × 50 g can anchovies, drained	*1 × 2 oz can anchovies, drained*

Preparation time: 10–15 minutes
Cooking time: about 15 minutes

Use new potatoes, scrubbed and diced, when they are available.

Cook the courgettes and the potatoes in salted boiling water until tender. Drain and dice the potatoes. Allow to cool. Combine the courgettes, potatoes and onion in a salad bowl. Place the eggs on top. Pour over the mayonnaise and garnish with the olives and a lattice of anchovies.

Cabbage with mustard soured cream dressing

Metric	Imperial
1 small white cabbage (about 450 g), cored and shredded	*1 small white cabbage (about 1 lb), cored and shredded*
150 ml soured cream	*¼ pint soured cream*
1 × 1.25 ml spoon dry mustard or 1 × 2.5 ml spoon made mustard	*¼ teaspoon dry mustard or ½ teaspoon made mustard*
1 × 15 ml spoon chopped fresh chives	*1 tablespoon chopped fresh chives*
1 × 5 ml spoon lemon juice	*1 teaspoon lemon juice*
sea salt	*sea salt*
freshly ground black pepper	*freshly ground black pepper*

Preparation time: 5–10 minutes

Put the cabbage into a bowl. Mix the remaining ingredients together with salt and pepper to taste, and toss with the cabbage. Serve at once.

Brown rice prawn salad

Metric	Imperial
175 g long-grain brown rice	*6 oz long-grain brown rice*
600 ml water	*1 pint water*
sea salt	*sea salt*
1 × 15 ml spoon sunflower oil	*1 tablespoon sunflower oil*
1 onion, peeled and finely chopped	*1 onion, peeled and finely chopped*
juice of ½ lemon	*juice of ½ lemon*
juice of ½ orange	*juice of ½ orange*
1 × 15 ml spoon tomato purée	*1 tablespoon tomato purée*
1 × 5 ml spoon paprika	*1 teaspoon paprika*
150 ml thick Mayonnaise (page 58)	*¼ pint thick Mayonnaise (page 58)*
100 g peeled prawns	*4 oz peeled prawns*
freshly ground black pepper	*freshly ground black pepper*
chopped fresh parsley, to garnish	*chopped fresh parsley, to garnish*

Preparation time: 10 minutes
Cooking time: 45 minutes, or 20 minutes if using a pressure cooker

Put the rice in a large saucepan with the water, 1 × 1.25 ml spoon/¼ teaspoon sea salt and the oil. Bring to the boil. Cook, uncovered, for 2 minutes, then stir once, cover tightly and simmer for 45 minutes (20 minutes if using a pressure cooker). When cooked, drain, rinse under running cold water and drain again thoroughly.
Stir the onion and lemon juice into the rice. Add the orange juice, tomato purée and paprika to the mayonnaise and mix well. Combine the prawns with the rice and onion and put in a serving dish. Taste and adjust the seasoning and pour over the mayonnaise. Sprinkle with parsley.

Courgette and potato salad; Cabbage with mustard soured cream dressing; Brown rice prawn salad

Braised vegetables with coriander

Metric
25 g butter
1 large onion, peeled and
  chopped
3 large heads of celery,
  trimmed and chopped
1 carrot, scraped and
  diced
1 parsnip, peeled and
  diced
300 ml chicken Stock
  (page 16) or water
2 × 15 ml spoons chopped
  fresh coriander leaves
  or 1 × 5 ml spoon
  ground coriander
pinch of dried thyme
1 × 15 ml spoon chopped
  fresh parsley
sea salt
freshly ground black
  pepper

To serve:
2 × 15 ml spoons double
  cream (optional)
1 × 15 ml spoon chopped
  fresh coriander leaves

Imperial
1 oz butter
1 large onion, peeled and
  chopped
3 large heads of celery,
  trimmed and chopped
1 carrot, scraped and
  diced
1 parsnip, peeled and
  diced
½ pint chicken Stock
  (page 16) or water
2 tablespoons chopped
  fresh coriander leaves
  or 1 teaspoon ground
  coriander
pinch of dried thyme
1 tablespoon chopped
  fresh parsley
sea salt
freshly ground black
  pepper

To serve:
2 tablespoons double
  cream (optional)
1 tablespoon chopped
  fresh coriander leaves

Preparation time: 10 minutes
Cooking time: 1 hour
Oven: 180°C, 350°F, Gas Mark 4

This dish goes particularly well with roast meat or chicken.

Melt the butter in a flameproof casserole or saucepan, add the onion and fry until transparent. Add the celery, carrot and parsnip and cook for 5 minutes. Pour over the stock or water and add the herbs and salt and pepper. Cover tightly and cook in a preheated oven for 1 hour. Alternatively, simmer the mixture on top of the stove for 1 hour.
Just before serving, strain off any excess juices and keep for making stock. Pour the cream over the vegetables, if used, and taste and adjust the seasoning. Sprinkle with fresh coriander leaves.

Ratatouille

Metric
1 large aubergine
sea salt
1½ × 15 ml spoons olive
  or nut oil
1 large onion, peeled and
  chopped
1 garlic clove, peeled
  and chopped
1 large green pepper,
  cored, seeded and diced
2 medium courgettes,
  thickly sliced
1 × 5 ml spoon dried basil
1 × 5 ml spoon dried
  marjoram
freshly ground black
  pepper
3 tomatoes, skinned and
  chopped, or 1 × 200 g
  can tomatoes
1 × 5 ml spoon tomato
  purée

Imperial
1 large aubergine
sea salt
1½ tablespoons olive or
  nut oil
1 large onion, peeled and
  chopped
1 garlic clove, peeled and
  chopped
1 large green pepper,
  cored, seeded and diced
2 medium courgettes,
  thickly sliced
1 teaspoon dried basil
1 teaspoon dried
  marjoram
freshly ground black
  pepper
3 tomatoes, skinned and
  chopped, or 1 × 7 oz
  can tomatoes
1 teaspoon tomato
  purée

Preparation time: 5–10 minutes, plus soaking
Cooking time: about 1 hour

This vegetable stew makes an excellent starter, served hot or cold. It forms a substantial vegetarian main course when served with potatoes or brown rice, or makes a good accompaniment to Chicken in a Brick with Lemon and Marjoram (page 48). Traditionally ratatouille is cooked for a long time to soften the vegetables and bring out the various flavours.

Slice the aubergine and put it in a colander. Sprinkle with salt and cover with a plate, weighted down. Leave for at least 30 minutes. Rinse the aubergine in cold water, drain on paper towels and dice.
Heat the oil in a large saucepan, add the onion and fry gently until transparent. Add the aubergine and when beginning to brown add the garlic. Add the green pepper and courgettes and cook for 5 minutes. Add the herbs, salt, pepper and the tomatoes. Cover tightly and simmer for 20 minutes, stirring occasionally. Stir in the tomato purée and simmer, covered, for 20 minutes. If the mixture is too liquid, reduce it by removing the lid for the last few minutes' cooking time. Taste and adjust the seasoning before serving.

Ratatouille;
Braised vegetables with coriander; Stuffed onions

Stuffed onions

Metric
4 medium onions, peeled
1 × 1.25 ml spoon dried
  sage
1 small apple, cored and
  grated
2 × 15 ml spoons fresh
  wholemeal breadcrumbs
2 walnuts, finely chopped
50 g Cheddar cheese,
  grated
sea salt
freshly ground black
  pepper
15 g butter

Imperial
4 medium onions, peeled
¼ teaspoon dried
  sage
1 small apple, cored and
  grated
2 tablespoons fresh
  wholemeal breadcrumbs
2 walnuts, finely chopped
2 oz Cheddar cheese,
  grated
sea salt
freshly ground black
  pepper
½ oz butter

Preparation time: 10 minutes
Cooking time: 50 minutes
Oven: 200°C, 400°F, Gas Mark 6

These stuffed onions go particularly well with pork.

Put the whole onions into a large saucepan, cover with cold water and bring to the boil. Simmer for 15–20 minutes. Drain the onions, reserving the cooking water for making stock.
Use a sharp pointed knife to cut away the tops of the onions, then scoop out their centres with a spoon. Chop the centres and mix with the sage, apple, breadcrumbs, walnuts, 25 g/1 oz of the cheese, and salt and pepper to taste. Use this mixture to stuff the onions.
Place the onions in a buttered ovenproof dish, top with the rest of the grated cheese and dot with the butter. Cook in a preheated oven for 30 minutes.

Lemon-glazed carrots

Metric	Imperial
750 g new carrots, lightly scraped	1½ lb new carrots, lightly scraped
juice of ½ lemon	juice of ½ lemon
1 × 2.5 ml spoon demerara sugar	½ teaspoon demerara sugar
15 g butter	½ oz butter

To serve:

15 g butter	½ oz butter
2 × 15 ml spoons chopped fresh parsley	2 tablespoons chopped fresh parsley

Preparation time: 5 minutes
Cooking time: about 20 minutes

If the carrots are large, slice them into thin rounds; if they are small, keep them whole. Put in a saucepan and pour over the lemon juice and just enough boiling water to cover. Add the sugar and butter, cover with a tightly fitting lid and simmer until the carrots are nearly tender. Remove the lid and allow the liquid to evaporate completely. Turn into a warmed serving dish, top with extra butter and sprinkle with parsley. Serve with Chicken in a Brick with Lemon and Marjoram (page 48).

Lemon-glazed carrots; Potatoes with parsley;
Broccoli with yogurt; Celeriac with lemon

Potatoes with parsley

Metric	Imperial
4 large potatoes, scrubbed	4 large potatoes, scrubbed
1 onion, peeled and finely chopped	1 onion, peeled and finely chopped
50 g butter, softened	2 oz butter, softened
large bunch of fresh parsley, finely chopped	large bunch of fresh parsley, finely chopped
50 g Cheddar or other hard cheese, grated (optional)	2 oz Cheddar or other hard cheese, grated (optional)
sea salt	sea salt
freshly ground black pepper	freshly ground black pepper

Preparation time: 5–10 minutes
Cooking time: about 1½ hours, depending on size of potatoes
Oven: 190°C, 375°F, Gas Mark 5

Without the grated cheese these potatoes are a delicious accompaniment to any roast meat or poultry. The parsley flavour also complements most fish dishes. Or serve them with Hamburgers (page 41) or a quiche, or a salad.

Bake the potatoes in a preheated oven for about 1¼ hours, or until they give to the touch. (A skewer through each potato shortens the cooking time.)
Meanwhile, combine the onion, butter, parsley, cheese, if used, and salt and pepper to taste.
When the potatoes are cooked, cut them in half lengthwise and scoop out the flesh, leaving the skins intact. Mix the cooked potato flesh with the parsley and onion mixture. Pile into the skins, return the potatoes to the dish and place in the oven for about 10 minutes to brown before serving.

Broccoli with yogurt

Metric
500 g broccoli
150 ml boiling water
1 × 2.5 ml spoon sea salt
2 × 5 ml spoons cornflour
2 × 15 ml spoons cold
  water
300 ml Natural Yogurt
  (page 8)
1 garlic clove, peeled and
  crushed
1 × 5 ml spoon dried mint
  or 3–4 fresh mint
  leaves, chopped
sea salt
freshly ground black
  pepper
15 g butter (optional)

Imperial
1¼ lb broccoli
¼ pint boiling water
½ teaspoon sea salt
2 teaspoons cornflour
2 tablespoons cold
  water
½ pint Natural Yogurt
  (page 8)
1 garlic clove, peeled and
  crushed
1 teaspoon dried mint, or
  3–4 fresh mint leaves,
  chopped
sea salt
freshly ground black
  pepper
½ oz butter (optional)

Preparation time: 5–10 minutes
Cooking time: 12–15 minutes

Put the broccoli in a saucepan and pour over the boiling water. Add the salt, cover with a tightly fitting lid and cook for 12–15 minutes, or until tender. Meanwhile, dissolve the cornflour in the cold water in a small pan. Stir in the yogurt, garlic, mint and salt and pepper to taste. Heat gently, stirring, until thickened. Whisk in the butter, if used.
When the broccoli is cooked, drain and put it into a warmed serving dish. Pour over the yogurt sauce and serve immediately.
This goes well with Hamburgers (page 41).

Celeriac with lemon

Metric
25 g butter
1 onion, peeled and
  chopped
1 head of celeriac (about
  500 g), cut into
  matchsticks
juice of ½ lemon
1 × 2.5 ml spoon
  demerara sugar
1 × 2.5 ml spoon dried
  marjoram
4 × 15 ml spoons Stock
  (page 16) or water
sea salt
freshly ground black
  pepper

Imperial
1 oz butter
1 onion, peeled and
  chopped
1 head of celeriac (about
  1¼ lb), cut into
  matchsticks
juice of ½ lemon
½ teaspoon demerara
  sugar
½ teaspoon dried
  marjoram
4 tablespoons Stock
  (page 16) or water
sea salt
freshly ground black
  pepper

Preparation time: 10 minutes
Cooking time: about 45 minutes

Melt the butter in a saucepan, add the onion and fry until transparent. Add the celeriac. Mix the lemon juice with the sugar and pour over the vegetables. Stir in the marjoram, stock or water and salt and pepper to taste.
Cover and simmer gently for about 45 minutes or until tender. If necessary add a little more stock or water during cooking.

Baked red cabbage

Metric	Imperial
25 g butter	1 oz butter
1 large onion, peeled and chopped	1 large onion, peeled and chopped
1 medium red cabbage, cored and finely shredded	1 medium red cabbage, cored and finely shredded
2 cloves	2 cloves
1 × 1.25 ml spoon grated nutmeg	¼ teaspoon grated nutmeg
1 × 1.25 ml spoon ground mixed spice	¼ teaspoon ground mixed spice
1 × 1.25 ml spoon ground cinnamon	¼ teaspoon ground cinnamon
1 × 1.25 ml spoon dry mustard	¼ teaspoon dry mustard
grated rind and juice of ½ lemon	grated rind and juice of ½ lemon
1 × 15 ml spoon dry sherry (optional)	1 tablespoon dry sherry (optional)
2 × 15 ml spoons clear honey	2 tablespoons clear honey
1 large cooking apple, peeled, cored and chopped	1 large cooking apple, peeled, cored and chopped
7 × 15 ml spoons apple juice	7 tablespoons apple juice

Preparation time: 10 minutes
Cooking time: 1 hour 5 minutes
Oven: 180°C, 350°F, Gas Mark 4

Melt the butter in a flameproof casserole, add the onion and gently fry until transparent. Add the shredded cabbage, cover tightly and cook gently for 5 minutes.

Meanwhile, mix together the cloves, nutmeg, mixed spice, cinnamon, mustard, lemon rind and juice, sherry, if used, and honey. Remove the casserole from the heat and stir in the spice mixture, apple and apple juice. Cover tightly and cook in a preheated oven for 1 hour. Taste and adjust the seasoning before serving.

Stir-fried cabbage

Metric	Imperial
4 × 15 ml spoons oil	4 tablespoons oil
1 onion, peeled and chopped	1 onion, peeled and chopped
1 garlic clove, peeled and chopped	1 garlic clove, peeled and chopped
1 × 2.5 cm piece root ginger, peeled and finely chopped	1 × 1 inch piece root ginger, peeled and finely chopped
1 medium green, white or red cabbage, cored and finely shredded	1 medium green, red or white cabbage, cored and finely shredded
1 × 5 ml spoon tomato purée	1 tablespoon tomato purée
1 × 15 ml spoon wine vinegar	1 tablespoon wine vinegar
2 drops Worcestershire sauce	2 drops Worcestershire sauce
2 drops Tabasco sauce	2 drops Tabasco sauce
sea salt	sea salt
1 × 15 ml spoon fresh marigold petals or 1½ × 5 ml spoons dried marigold petals (optional)	1 tablespoon fresh marigold petals or 1½ teaspoons dried marigold petals (optional)

Preparation time: 5 minutes
Cooking time: about 20 minutes

Marigold petals are available from health food shops.

Heat the oil in a deep, heavy-based pan or a wok, add the onion and fry until browned. Add the garlic and ginger and fry for a further 2 minutes. Add the shredded cabbage and continue cooking for a further 5 minutes, stirring frequently.

Stir the tomato purée into the wine vinegar and pour over the cabbage. Add the Worcestershire and Tabasco sauce, salt to taste and the marigold petals, if using. Cook for about 10 minutes, stirring frequently, until the cabbage is tender but still firm.

Serve with Spare Ribs with Ginger (page 39).

Cauliflower with garlic and almonds

Metric	Imperial
1 large cauliflower, cut into florets	*1 large cauliflower, cut into florets*
40 g butter	*1½ oz butter*
4 × 15 ml spoons fresh wholemeal breadcrumbs	*4 tablespoons fresh wholemeal breadcrumbs*
25 g flaked almonds	*1 oz flaked almonds*
1 garlic clove, peeled and finely chopped	*1 garlic clove, peeled and finely chopped*
sea salt	*sea salt*
freshly ground black pepper	*freshly ground black pepper*
chopped fresh parsley, to garnish	*chopped fresh parsley, to garnish*

Baked red cabbage; Stir-fried cabbage; Cauliflower with garlic and almonds

Preparation time: 5–10 minutes
Cooking time: about 10 minutes

Cook the cauliflower florets in a little boiling salted water for about 10 minutes.

Meanwhile, melt the butter in a frying pan and fry the breadcrumbs with the almonds and garlic until well browned. Add salt and pepper and remove the pan from the heat.

When the cauliflower is cooked, drain and arrange the florets in a warmed buttered serving dish. Scatter over the breadcrumb mixture, sprinkle with parsley and serve immediately.

This is a good vegetable dish to serve with Mackerel with Gooseberry Sauce (page 53).

Serves 6

PUDDINGS AND DESSERTS

The healthiest dessert includes fresh fruit. All fruits contain varying amounts of vitamin C and they are a source of natural sugar. Fruit fools can be whisked together in a few minutes. A purée of fruit can be sweetened with raw sugar (page 4) or clear honey and mixed with whipped cream, or Natural Yogurt (page 8) for half the cream. If using fresh apricots, plums, rhubarb and gooseberries these should be cooked in a little water before puréeing. Dried prunes or apricots can be prepared similarly, but they should be soaked and cooked first.

For a fruit syllabub use half white wine and half whipped cream, and fold in two stiffly beaten egg whites. Fruit syllabub should be chilled for 2–3 hours and in this time the mixture will separate, unlike the smooth thick fruit-based fools.

There are occasions, however, when a warming, hot pudding is wanted. With a little thought most recipes can be adapted to include wholegrain or unrefined ingredients, such as nuts, honey and wholemeal flour, as the ideas here illustrate.

Vanilla sugar is used in many of these desserts. To prepare a quantity for general use, break a vanilla pod into pieces and bury these into about 450 g/1 lb of any raw sugar (page 4) in an airtight jar.

Hazelnut pie; Almond curd cheese

Almond curd cheese

Metric	Imperial
450 g curd cheese	1 lb curd cheese
3 egg yolks	3 egg yolks
50 g ground almonds	2 oz ground almonds
50 g demerara sugar	2 oz demerara sugar
25 g demerara Vanilla Sugar (page 70)	1 oz demerara Vanilla Sugar (page 70)
1 × 1.25 ml spoon almond essence	½ teaspoon almond essence
2 × 15 ml spoons brandy (other liqueur may be substituted)	2 tablespoons brandy (other liqueur may be substituted)
flaked almonds, to decorate	flaked almonds, to decorate

Preparation time: 5 minutes, plus 2–3 hours for chilling

Serve this dessert with Ammaretti di Saronno biscuits: these are almond-flavoured macaroons and are available from delicatessen shops. Alternatively, use the three remaining egg whites to make Demerara Meringues (page 76), and hand these round separately. If you do not have demerara vanilla sugar use 100 g/4 oz demerara sugar and 1 × 5 ml spoon/1 teaspoon vanilla essence.

Combine all the ingredients in a large mixing bowl and beat until smooth. Pour into a serving dish, or individual glasses, and chill in the refrigerator for 2–3 hours until set. Decorate with almonds.

Variation:

For a cheesecake pudding (less rich) pour the mixture into a greased and floured 15 cm/6 inch loose-bottomed cake tin and bake in the centre of a preheated oven (120°C, 250°F, Gas Mark ½) for 2 hours. Allow the cake to cool completely in the tin.

Hazelnut pie

Metric	Imperial
175 g plain wholemeal flour	6 oz plain wholemeal flour
75 g fat (butter or vegetable margarine, or a mixture of both)	3 oz fat (butter or vegetable margarine, or a mixture of both)
2–3 × 15 ml spoons cold water	2–3 tablespoons cold water
chopped hazelnuts, to garnish (optional)	chopped hazelnuts, to garnish (optional)

Filling:	Filling:
2 eggs	2 eggs
1 egg yolk	1 egg yolk
150 g Barbados sugar	5 oz Barbados sugar
100 g butter, melted	4 oz butter, melted
150 ml Natural Yogurt (page 8)	¼ pint Natural Yogurt (page 8)
100 g ground hazelnuts	4 oz ground hazelnuts

Preparation time: 15 minutes, plus 30 minutes for chilling
Cooking time: 1 hour
Oven: 200°C, 400°F, Gas Mark 6; 180°C, 350°F, Gas Mark 4

Put the flour in a bowl and rub in the fat until the mixture resembles breadcrumbs. Gradually add the water and mix to a firm dough. Chill the dough for at least 30 minutes.

Roll out the dough and line a 20–23 cm/8–9 inch flan tin. Bake blind in a preheated oven for 15 minutes. Remove the paper and beans and prick the pastry base with a fork. Reduce the oven temperature and bake for a further 10 minutes. Cool.

Whisk together the eggs, egg yolk and sugar. Add the melted butter and yogurt and whisk until well blended. Scatter the ground nuts over the bottom of the pastry case and pour over the yogurt mixture.

Bake the flan in a preheated oven for 30–35 minutes or until the filling is firm to the touch. If using, sprinkle with chopped hazelnuts. Serve warm, with cream.

Pear nut crumble

Metric	Imperial
3–4 large pears, about 750 g, peeled, cored and roughly chopped	3–4 large pears, about 1½ lb, peeled, cored and roughly chopped
4 × 15 ml spoons Barbados sugar	4 tablespoons Barbados sugar
150 g plain wholemeal flour	5 oz plain wholemeal flour
1 × 2.5 ml spoon ground cardamom (optional)	½ teaspoon ground cardamom (optional)
1 × 2.5 ml spoon ground mixed spice	½ teaspoon ground mixed spice
1 × 5 ml spoon ground cinnamon	1 teaspoon ground cinnamon
1 × 1.25 ml spoon grated nutmeg	¼ teaspoon grated nutmeg
75 g butter, softened	3 oz butter, softened
50 g Brazil nuts, chopped	2 oz Brazil nuts, chopped

Preparation time: 10–15 minutes
Cooking time: 35 minutes
Oven: 200°C, 400°F, Gas Mark 6

Put the pears in a bowl, sprinkle with 1 × 15 ml spoon/1 tablespoon of the sugar and set aside.

Mix the flour and spices together in a large mixing bowl and rub in the butter until the mixture resembles fine breadcrumbs. Stir in the remaining sugar.

Line the bottom of a buttered ovenproof dish with one-third of the crumble mixture. Put half the pears and any juice on top. Sprinkle with half of the remaining crumble mixture, cover with the rest of the pears and juice and sprinkle with a final layer of crumble mixture. Scatter over the Brazil nuts.

Cover with foil and bake in a preheated oven for 35 minutes, removing the foil for the last 10 minutes. Serve hot, with Demerara Custard (page 73).

Variation:
Make this crumble with eating apples, or peaches, when they are in season.

Baked apples with blackcurrants

Metric	Imperial
4 large cooking apples, cored	4 large cooking apples, cored
225 g fresh blackcurrants	8 oz fresh blackcurrants
5 × 15 ml spoons clear honey	5 tablespoons clear honey
150 ml boiling water	¼ pint boiling water
4 × 15 ml spoons demerara sugar	4 tablespoons demerara sugar
50 g butter (optional)	2 oz butter (optional)

Preparation time: 5–10 minutes
Cooking time: 45 minutes
Oven: 180°C, 350°F, Gas Mark 4

With the point of a sharp knife slit the apple skin all round the middle, then put the apples into an ovenproof dish. Fill each core cavity with the fresh blackcurrants, scattering any leftover blackcurrants in the dish. Stir the honey into the boiling water and pour over the stuffed apples. Sprinkle with the sugar and dot each apple with butter, if using.

Bake in a preheated oven for 45 minutes or until cooked. Serve hot or cold, with cream, Natural Yogurt (page 8) or Demerara Custard (page 73).

Variations:
Fill the apples with fresh blackberries or cranberries. Fill the apples with chopped mixed dried fruit, and pour over apple or fresh orange juice, sweetened with a little honey, to taste.

Pear nut crumble; Baked apples with blackcurrants; Brown rice pudding; Demerara custard

Brown rice pudding

Metric	Imperial
75 g short-grain brown rice	3 oz short-grain brown rice
600 ml milk	1 pint milk
50 g Barbados sugar, preferably Vanilla Sugar (page 70)	2 oz Barbados sugar, preferably Vanilla Sugar (page 70)
1 × 5 ml spoon vanilla essence (if vanilla sugar is not available)	1 teaspoon vanilla essence (if vanilla sugar is not available)
1 × 1.25 ml spoon sea salt	¼ teaspoon sea salt
1 × 15 ml spoon sherry (optional)	1 tablespoon sherry (optional)

Preparation time: 5 minutes
Cooking time: 3 hours
Oven: 140°C, 275°F, Gas Mark 1

Put the rice into a buttered 600 ml/1 pint ovenproof dish. Put all the other ingredients into a large saucepan and bring to the boil, stirring. Pour the flavoured milk over the rice.
Bake in a preheated oven for 3 hours. To prevent a brown skin forming, cover with buttered greaseproof paper for the first 2 hours. Serve hot or cold, with Dried Fruit Compôte, (page 8). In the summer, serve this pudding cold with fresh raspberries and single cream.

Variations:
Lemon Rice Pudding: omit the sherry and include the thinly-pared rind of ½ lemon.
Spicy Rice Pudding: omit the sherry and flavour the milk with 1 × 2.5 ml spoon/½ teaspoon each of ground mixed spice, ground cinnamon and grated nutmeg.

Demerara custard

Metric	Imperial
300 ml milk	½ pint milk
2 × 15 ml spoons, demerara sugar preferably Vanilla Sugar (page 70)	2 tablespoons demerara sugar, preferably Vanilla Sugar (page 70)
3 drops vanilla essence (if vanilla sugar is not available)	3 drops vanilla essence (if vanilla sugar is not available)
2 egg yolks	2 egg yolks

Preparation time: 10 minutes
Cooking time: 10 minutes

Commercial custard powder is a blend of starch, colouring and synthetic flavouring, whereas this recipe provides a wholesome, delicious sauce for winter puddings. It can also make a quick dessert on its own, topped with chopped dried fruit or nuts.

Heat the milk with the sugar and vanilla essence, if used, in a double boiler or in a heatproof bowl over a pan of boiling water. In a separate bowl beat the egg yolks until pale in colour.
When the milk just starts to boil, pour it slowly over the yolks, beating all the time. Beat well, then pour the mixture back into the double boiler or bowl over the hot water. Heat very gently, stirring continuously until thickened. Do not allow the mixture to boil.

Fresh pineapple and soured cream flan

Preparation time: 20 minutes
Cooking time: 30 minutes
Oven: 180°C, 350°F, Gas Mark 4

Metric
175 g digestive biscuits, crushed
75 g butter, melted
1 × 5 ml spoon ground cinnamon
1 × 5 ml spoon Barbados sugar

Filling:
225 g curd cheese
3 × 15 ml spoons clear honey or demerara sugar
150 ml soured cream
1 egg yolk
1 small ripe fresh pineapple, peeled, cut into chunks and drained of excess juice
150 ml double or whipping cream, whipped, to decorate

Imperial
6 oz digestive biscuits, crushed
3 oz butter, melted
1 teaspoon ground cinnamon
1 teaspoon Barbados sugar

Filling:
8 oz curd cheese
3 tablespoons clear honey or demerara sugar
¼ pint soured cream
1 egg yolk
1 small ripe fresh pineapple, peeled, cut into chunks and drained of excess juice
¼ pint double or whipping cream, whipped, to decorate

The curd cheese and soured cream custard base sets off the natural sweetness of fresh pineapple, which should need no added sugar.

Mix together the biscuit crumbs, melted butter, cinnamon and sugar. Press the mixture over the bottom and sides of a greased 20–23 cm/8–9 inch flan dish and smooth with the back of a spoon.
Whisk together the curd cheese, honey or sugar, soured cream and egg yolk. When thoroughly mixed pour over the biscuit base. Bake in a preheated oven for 30 minutes or until the custard is lightly set. Allow to cool.
Cover the top with the chunks of fresh pineapple and decorate with whipped cream. Alternatively the whipped cream may be handed round separately.

Variation:
Substitute seedless grapes, stoned cherries or fresh strawberries for the pineapple. Don't use canned fruit, but choose any fresh fruit that is in season. If it is not as sweet as pineapple, sprinkle with a little demerara sugar.

Vanilla ice cream

Preparation time: 10 minutes
Cooking time: 5 minutes

Metric	*Imperial*
300 ml single cream or milk	½ pint single cream or milk
4 egg yolks	4 egg yolks
75 g Barbados Vanilla Sugar (page 70)	3 oz Barbados Vanilla Sugar (page 70)
300 ml double or whipping cream, lightly whipped	½ pint double or whipping cream, lightly whipped

The best ice cream is made with all cream, as milk does tend to form a more watery, granular ice. However, if you want to cut cost, calories and cholesterol, use a mixture of double cream and milk. Home-made ice cream makes a rich, delicious dessert – serve it occasionally as a treat.

This custard should be sweeter than for a pouring custard, but do not oversweeten it, as too much sugar inhibits freezing. Turn the refrigerator to its lowest setting about 1 hour before preparing the ice cream. Alternatively use a freezer.

Bring the single cream or milk to the boil in a heavy based saucepan or in a double boiler. In a bowl stir together the egg yolks and vanilla sugar. Pour the boiling cream or milk over the yolk mixture, stirring constantly. Strain the mixture back into the saucepan and stir over a very gentle heat until thickened. This should only take a couple of minutes and the custard must not boil, or it will curdle. Turn into a large bowl and allow to cool.

Fold in the cream. Place in the freezing compartment of the refrigerator or in the freezer, and freeze for 1 hour or until the mixture is starting to crystallize.

Remove the ice cream and whisk briskly for 1–2 minutes. (This ensures a smooth ice cream, but is not absolutely necessary with this rich recipe.) Put the ice cream into a plastic container, cover and return to the freezing compartment or freezer. Freeze for at least 2 hours.

Leave to soften at room temperature for 15 minutes before serving, with wafers or with small Demerara Meringues (page 76).

Makes 600 ml/1 pint

Variations:

Coffee Ice Cream: Dissolve 2 × 15 ml spoons/2 tablespoons instant coffee powder in 1 × 15 ml spoon/1 tablespoon boiling water, with 1 × 15 ml spoon/1 tablespoon Barbados sugar. Stir this into the cooled custard, before folding in the whipped cream. Add 2 × 15 ml spoons/2 tablespoons Tia Maria for a really luxurious taste.

Fig and Port Ice Cream: Soak 225 g/8 oz dried figs (about 14 figs) overnight, in just enough water to cover. The next day, drain the fruit and reserve the juice for drinking. Chop the soaked figs, removing any hard stalks, and add to the cooled custard together with 2 × 15 ml spoons/2 tablespoons port or sherry. Alternatively, blend the figs to a purée in a liquidizer, with the port or sherry, and then add to the custard.

Apricot and Port Ice Cream: Substitute 225 g/8 oz dried apricots for figs and follow the fig and port recipe above.

Fresh pineapple and soured cream flan; Apricot and port ice cream; Coffee ice cream

BAKING

Baking with whole grain flour and sweeteners such as honey, molasses and brown sugars presents a deliciously healthy style of cooking. Many cake recipes can be adapted to include unrefined ingredients and the recipes here also includes most and fresh fruit, and nuts.

Most of these cakes are made from wheatmeal flour. For a slightly coarser texture wholemeal flour can be substituted. However, if you do this the quantity of liquid may need to be increased slightly, depending on the absorbency of the flour, which can vary.

Nearly all cakes contain fat in one form or another. Although they supply vitamins A, D and E, it is best to eat all fats in moderation, keeping those tecipes high in fat for special occasions.

Demerara meringues

Metric	*Imperial*
2 egg whites	*2 egg whites*
100 g demerara sugar	*4 oz demerara sugar*

Preparation time: 10 minutes
Cooking time: 2 hours, plus overnight drying
Oven: 120°C, 250°F, Gas Mark ½

This recipe is a good way of using up egg whites left over from making desserts and sauces. These meringues are crisp on the outside, with chewy centres, and they do not have the cloying sweetness of meringues made with white refined sugar.

Beat the egg whites until stiff. Add 50 g/2 oz of the sugar and continue beating for 1 minute. Lightly fold in the remaining sugar, using a metal spoon.

Pipe or spoon the meringue mixture on to a baking sheet lined with oiled greaseproof paper. Bake on a low shelf in a preheated oven for 2 hours. Gently turn the meringues on their sides, switch off the oven and leave the meringues to dry out overnight.

Sandwich the meringues together with whipped cream, or serve with ice cream or Almond Curd Cheese (page 71). These meringues can be stored in an airtight container for up to 5 days.

Makes 12–16

Banana cake

Metric
100 g self-raising
   wheatmeal flour
100 g butter, softened
100 g Barbados sugar
2 eggs (size 1 or 2)
   beaten
2 ripe bananas, peeled
   and mashed
1 × 2.5 ml spoon baking
   powder
a little icing sugar, to
   finish

Imperial
4 oz self-raising
   wheatmeal flour
4 oz butter, softened
4 oz Barbados sugar
2 eggs (size 1 or 2)
   beaten
2 ripe bananas, peeled
   and mashed
½ teaspoon baking powder
a little icing sugar, to
   finish

Filling:
225 g curd cheese
1 × 2.5 ml spoon lemon
   juice
about 2 × 15 ml spoons
   thick honey
1 large banana, peeled
   and thinly sliced

Filling:
8 oz curd cheese
½ teaspoon lemon
   juice
about 2 tablespoons
   thick honey
1 large banana, peeled
   and thinly sliced

Preparation time: 15–20 minutes
Cooking time: 30–40 minutes
Oven: 180°C, 350°F, Gas Mark 4

This cake is best eaten as fresh as possible. If you want to make and fill it in advance, keep it in the refrigerator, or bake the cake and store it in an airtight container until required, then spread with the filling just before serving. Sieved cottage cheese can be substituted for the curd cheese.

Sift the flour into a bowl, tipping in any bran left in the sieve. Set aside. Cream the butter with the sugar in another mixing bowl until the mixture is fluffy. Beat in the eggs a little at a time, adding 1 × 15 ml spoon/1 tablespoon of the sifted flour after each addition. Fold in the rest of the flour with a metal spoon.
Combine the mashed bananas with the baking powder, then fold into the cake mixture. Mix thoroughly, but do not beat as this would remove the air already incorporated and might make the cake crack.
Divide the mixture between two greased and lined 18 cm/7 inch sandwich tins and smooth the tops. Bake in a preheated oven for 30–40 minutes, or until the cakes are springy to the touch. Cool on a wire tray.
To make the filling, beat together the curd cheese, lemon juice and honey. Spread this over one cake layer and top with the sliced banana. Place the other cake half on top and dust with sifted icing sugar.
Makes one 18 cm/7 inch round cake

Carrot and almond cake

Metric
5 eggs, separated
200 g demerara sugar
grated rind of ½ orange
275 g carrots, peeled and
   grated
275 g ground almonds
100 g plain wheatmeal
   sifted
1 × 15 ml spoon brandy or
   orange liqueur (Grand
   Marnier) or orange
   juice

Imperial
5 eggs, separated
7 oz demerara sugar
grated rind of ½ orange
10 oz carrots, peeled and
   grated
10 oz ground almonds
4 oz plain wheatmeal,
   sifted
1 tablespoon brandy or
   orange liqueur (Grand
   Marnier) or orange
   juice

To finish:
2 × 15 ml spoons
   demerara sugar
1 × 5 ml spoon ground
   cinnamon
25 g flaked almonds

To finish:
2 tablespoons
   demerara sugar
1 teaspoon ground
   cinnamon
1 oz flaked almonds

Preparation time: 20 minutes
Cooking time: 1 hour
Oven: 190°C, 375°F, Gas Mark 5

This substantial cake is kept beautifully moist by the grated carrots. Store the cake in an airtight container in the refrigerator if intending to leave it for more than 3 days.

Beat the egg yolks with a wire whisk until frothy. Gradually add the sugar and beat until the mixture is pale and thick. Fold in the orange rind, carrots, almonds, flour and brandy, liqueur or orange juice. Beat the egg whites until stiff and fold into the cake mixture with a metal spoon. Pour the mixture into a greased and floured 18 cm/7 inch square tin.
Mix together the demerara sugar and cinnamon and sprinkle over the surface. Scatter the flaked almonds on top. Bake in the centre of a preheated oven for 1 hour or until the cake is springy to the touch and a hot skewer inserted into the centre comes out clean. Leave the cake to cool in the tin for about 15 minutes before turning it out on to a wire tray to cool.
Makes one 18 cm/7 inch square cake

Variation:
A more economical version of this cake can be made by reducing the ground almonds to 100 g/4 oz and increasing the flour to 275 g/10 oz, and the carrots to 350 g/12 oz. Add two drops of almond essence with the liqueur or orange juice and make the cake in exactly the same way as described above.

Banana cake; Demerara meringues; Carrot and almond cake

Treacle and sultana flapjacks

Preparation time: 10 minutes
Cooking time: 40 minutes
Oven: 160°C, 325°F, Gas Mark 3

Metric	Imperial
150 g butter or vegetable margarine	5 oz butter or vegetable margarine
75 g Barbados or molasses sugar	3 oz Barbados or molasses sugar
1–2 × 15 ml spoons black molasses	1–2 tablespoons black molasses
50 g sultanas	2 oz sultanas
225 g jumbo or rolled oats	8 oz jumbo or rolled oats
grated rind and juice of ½ lemon	grated rind and juice of ½ lemon

Melt the butter or margarine in a saucepan. Stir in the sugar and molasses. Add the sultanas, oats and lemon rind and juice and mix well. Press the mixture into a greased 25 × 20 cm/10 × 8 inch tin.
Bake in a preheated oven for 40 minutes. Allow to cool for 10 minutes, then cut into bars. Leave in the tin until completely cold.
Makes 12

Wholemeal chocolate cake

Preparation time: 30 minutes
Cooking time: 35 minutes
Oven: 180°C, 350°F, Gas Mark 4

Metric	Imperial
100 g self-raising wheatmeal flour	4 oz self-raising wheatmeal flour
1 × 5 ml spoon baking powder	1 teaspoon baking powder
100 g Barbados sugar	4 oz Barbados sugar
100 g soft (tub) margarine	4 oz soft (tub) margarine
1 × 15 ml spoon milk	1 tablespoon milk
2 eggs (size 1 or 2)	2 eggs (size 1 or 2)
50 g plain chocolate, melted	2 oz plain chocolate, melted

Filling:

Metric	Imperial
50 g plain chocolate, broken into small pieces	2 oz plain chocolate, broken into small pieces
3 × 15 ml spoons clear honey	3 tablespoons clear honey
50 g butter	2 oz butter
2 × 15 ml spoons low fat powdered milk	2 tablespoons low fat powdered milk
1 × 15 ml spoon cold water	1 tablespoon cold water

Topping (optional):

Metric	Imperial
100 g plain chocolate, broken into small pieces	4 oz plain chocolate, broken into small pieces
2 × 15 ml spoons rum or water	2 tablespoons rum or water
6 walnut halves	6 walnut halves

This chocolate cake is whisked together in minutes, and it has a delicious chocolate butter filling, sweetened with honey. If preferred sprinkle the top with vanilla-flavoured icing sugar.

Sift the flour and baking powder into a large mixing bowl and tip in any bran left in the sieve. Add the sugar, margarine and milk and beat thoroughly for 1 minute. (This is best done with an electric mixer, at top speed.) Add the eggs and chocolate and continue beating for 1 minute, occasionally scraping the mixture away from the sides of the bowl.
Divide the mixture between two greased and lined 18 cm/7 inch sandwich tins and smooth the tops. Bake in a preheated oven for 35 minutes or until a hot skewer inserted into the centres comes out clean. Leave to cool in the tins for about 30 seconds, then turn out on to a wire tray to cool completely.
To make the filling, put the chocolate, honey and butter in a heavy-based saucepan and melt gently, stirring. Remove from the heat. Dissolve the powdered milk in the cold water and stir into the chocolate butter. Leave the mixture to cool completely and thicken, then use it to sandwich the cakes together.
To make the topping, melt the chocolate with the rum or water in a heatproof bowl over a pan of hot water. Allow to cool slightly, then pour the mixture over the cake, smoothing it over the top and down the sides with a palette knife dipped in hot water. Decorate with the walnut halves. Leave to cool and set.
Makes one 18 cm/7 inch cake

Variations:
Use 25 g/1 oz Vanilla Sugar (page 70) and 75 g/3 oz Barbados sugar in the cake.
Add 15 g/½ oz walnuts, chopped, to the cake mixture before baking.

Spicy apple, date and sesame loaf

Preparation time: 15–20 minutes
Cooking time: $1\frac{1}{2}$–$1\frac{3}{4}$ hours
Oven: 160°C, 325°F, Gas Mark 3

Metric	Imperial
350 g self-raising wheatmeal flour	12 oz self-raising wheatmeal flour
1 × 1.25 ml spoon fine sea salt	$\frac{1}{4}$ teaspoon fine sea salt
1 × 1.25 ml spoon grated nutmeg	$\frac{1}{4}$ teaspoon grated nutmeg
1 × 1.25 ml spoon ground allspice	$\frac{1}{4}$ teaspoon ground allspice
1 × 1.25 ml spoon ground mace	$\frac{1}{4}$ teaspoon ground mace
1 × 1.25 ml spoon ground cardamom	$\frac{1}{4}$ teaspoon ground cardamom
1 × 1.25 ml spoon ground ginger	$\frac{1}{4}$ teaspoon ground ginger
1 × 5 ml spoon ground cinnamon	1 teaspoon ground cinnamon
grated rind of $\frac{1}{2}$ lemon	grated rind of $\frac{1}{2}$ lemon
50 g Barbados or molasses sugar	2 oz Barbados or molasses sugar
2 eggs (size 1 or 2), beaten	2 eggs (size 1 or 2), beaten
150 ml Natural Yogurt (page 8)	$\frac{1}{4}$ pint Natural Yogurt (page 8)
1 large cooking apple, peeled, cored and grated	1 large cooking apple, peeled, cored and grated
225 g stoned dates, chopped	8 oz stoned dates, chopped
50 g sesame seeds	2 oz sesame seeds

If you prefer, use 1 × 5 ml spoon/1 teaspoon ground mixed spice instead of the allspice, mace, cardamom and ginger.

Sift the flour, salt and spices into a large mixing bowl, tipping in any bran left in the sieve. Stir in the lemon rind and sugar and make a well in the centre. Pour in the eggs and yogurt and gradually mix the dry ingredients into the liquid. Stir in the apple, dates and 25 g/ 1 oz of the sesame seeds.

Shape the mixture into a loaf and put into a well-greased and lightly floured 1 kg/2 lb loaf tin. Press down the corners and smooth the top with the back of a spoon. Scatter over the rest of the sesame seeds and press them into the top of the loaf.

Bake in the centre of a preheated oven for $1\frac{1}{2}$–$1\frac{3}{4}$ hours until well-risen and lightly browned. Allow the loaf to cool in the tin for 5–10 minutes before turning it out on to a wire tray to cool completely. Store for at least 1 day before serving, sliced and buttered.

Makes one 1 kg/2 lb loaf

Variations:

For 100 g/4 oz of the dates, substitute 100 g/4 oz glacé cherries, chopped, or 100 g/4 oz walnuts, chopped.

Spicy apple, date and sesame loaf;
Wholemeal chocolate cake; Treacle and sultana flapjacks

INDEX